Co

Croatia Strikes Back

Cody McClain Brown

Croatia Strikes Back: The Unnecessary Sequel
Copyright © Cody McClain Brown 2018

Cover design by Kristina Musić

2nd edition

CODY MCCLAIN BROWN

CROATIA STRIKES BACK

CONTENTS

PROLOGUE
Without a name or dimension ---------------------------------9

CHAPTER 1
It takes a cyber village to feel at home-----------------------15

CHAPTER 2
Boredom, the great breeding ground of friendship -----23

CHAPTER 3
Flying Kid Kicks at Midnight ---------------------------------29

CHAPTER 4
Punica's house is wherever punica is -------------------------37

CHAPTER 5
The Missing Chapter--45

CHAPTER 6
The Hardest Hope --51

CHAPTER 7
Too much chocolate --61

CHAPTER 8
Buying an apartment is... difficult ----------------------------69

CHAPTER 9
A Real Friend Is a Skeptic-------------------------------------80

CHAPTER 10
Missing America --92

CHAPTER 11
Learning Croatian ---99

CHAPTER 12
The healthcare is (almost) free ---------------------------------123

CHAPTER 13
Moving is as painful as childbirth? ----------------------------130

CHAPTER 14
Bureaucracy! The never ending nightmare -----------------142

CHAPTER 15
The biggest difference between here and there ---------154

CHAPTER 16
Questions about America---162

CHAPTER 17
How to play "Croatia the Board Game" ---------------------170

CHAPTER 18
Boba Fetch and Tomorrow ---------------------------------------177

For our neighbors, you are certainly worth the move.

PROLOGUE
Without a name or dimension

A few years ago, I missed my daughter's birth...

It's about 8:30 AM and I wake up. For the past month I've slept with my cellphone right beside my bed, plugged in, waiting for an urgent text from my wife Vana. This morning, still groggy, I flip open my phone and there it is: nine month's worth of anticipation waiting for me on the cracked screen of an old Motorola.

"I'm at the hospital," is all it says. I'm up! Shooting, leaping out of bed, but tangled in the sheets. Tripping, I hop down the hall, dragging the sheets with me into the living room. Why am I not getting dressed? Why am I not racing to the hospital? I run to my desk and open my laptop because I'm in Kansas and my wife is about to give birth in Split, Croatia!

I launch Skype and dial the number. It rings and rings and I worry, *is she already giving birth? Am I a dad? Is she OK? Are they OK? What's happening!?!*

Finally she answers. Her voice is a bit panicked, but still calm. I ask a billion questions into the wallpaper on my laptop.

"Love, love," she says. "I'm about to go in."

"You're going to give birth today? Now?"

"I-I think so." I hear the worry fade, I imagine a smile resting on her voice.

"Wow," is all I can say.

"I gotta go."

"OK. I love you."

"I ja tebe, ljubavi."

I don't know what else to say, but I want to say something.

"Don't worry!" I blurt out unsure if she hears me before the connection is lost.

I have no idea what I do for the next few hours or minutes. Time just seems... not to stop, but to disappear. Finally, I decide to call my mother-in-law, punica[1], to check-in.

"ALLO?" She yells through the tiny speakers on my laptop. I can hear the rush of traffic from a nearby street coming through the kitchen window of her apartment. I imagine it's evening there, and warm. A scooter whines through our connection *(Sigh), Split*.

"Vida?" I say. "CO-DY JE NA TELE-FON-U!" (this is translated from Croatian as, Vida, Cody is on the phone. As if she couldn't tell from my accent). Vida yells something back. All I can make out are the words I know.

"HOSPITAL!"

"VANA!"

"BABY!"

---

[1] Pronounced *poo-ni-tsa*, *punica* is the Croatian word for a husband's mother-in-law.

Because my Croatian is so bad I have no idea what order any of this should go in. Has the baby arrived? Or are we still waiting? Is Vida telling me what I already know, or is there some new information I need to decode in all of this? I yell back in my best Croatian something that probably sounds like this:

"BABY ARRIVED HAS?"

"NO! NOT YET!"

"ME CALL ITSELF TO YOU AGAIN!" I scream at my keyboard.

"OK," punica yells back to me.

And this goes on a few more times before I finally dial back and manage to get the message.

"BEBA JE DOŠLA!" (The baby has arrived).

"OK THEY?" I ask.

"ALL OK." Then punica begins to give me the measurements, but since it's all in Croatian as well as metric measurements (which we still don't use in the US) she might as well be telling it to me in *two* foreign languages. *Goddam American exceptionalism!* She keeps going, telling me my daughter is 3 pounds or 13 pounds or 10 kilos or is it 345 kilos? *How much is 345 kilos? Is it kilo then grams? Is that more or less than one pound? How much is any of that?* I mean I don't even know what a baby is supposed to weigh. I'm completely lost here. And she's saying she's 50 centimeters long, which sounds like half a meter, and that's a yard, I think. But is that right? An American football field is only 200 babies long? I'm all confused, but happy that everyone seems all right.

I ask if she thinks I should call Vana. But, I don't know if she understands what I'm saying because I don't even know if I said what I wanted to say. Finally, we end the "conversation" and I decide to call my wife's sister. In calm, accented English, she tells me everything is fine. At some point I get Vana on the phone and she sounds good, but then I hear her say something in a voice I've never heard her use before. It's a soft, sweet voice and I realize this new voice is the wonderful voice she is using to talk to our daughter. At once I feel as close and distant as ever, and then it hits me what we've done. We're no longer a married couple. We're parents.

Throughout the day I keep running into people and sharing with them the good news. I must sound a bit mad.

"My wife just gave birth!" I announce.

"Congratulations! Boy? Girl?"

"It's a girl!"

"What's her name?"

"Um... well..." We hadn't decided on a name. Each time we came up with a name we both liked, my mother-in-law or one of the neighbors in Split would veto it. Usually with some story about someone *they* had known with that name and how that person was shifty, crazy or *had issues* or something. We also needed something that could be transatlantic. You know, something that translated well. Names that I loved in Croatia, like *Jadranka* were off the list because *Jadranka* in America becomes *Ya Dranka*, like "Ya Dranka all that there tequila?"[2]

Now, people who have had babies, I guess other parents, usually want to know how big your baby is when you tell them you've just had a baby. The stats for weight and size

---

[2] The worse name for this is Jerko. Pronounced Yerko in Croatian, in English it becomes, well Jerk-O. I know a guy with this name who was unfortunate enough to study in Arkansas.

are the baby equivalent to the stats for baskets, goals or runs of a professional athlete. But whenever anyone asks me, "How big is what's-her-name?" I'm at a loss.

"Um... well..." and I explain how it's all in Croatian and European math. So in more ways than one, my daughter was born into the world without a name or dimension.

Five years later and Sara has a name, it's um... Sara. We are going to *Narodne novine*, which translates as the "People's Papers." I think it's a holdover name from socialism. The whole way there I'm thinking about how I can ask the seller for colored paper because that's what Sara wants us to buy. The last time we were there all I could find by myself was the more expensive fluorescent printer paper. I really don't want to buy that. It's pricey, only comes in packs of 200 sheets, and is so bright that I worry if Sara gets it all our retinas will burn out from looking at all the colored stars she cuts out and tapes all over the room all the time. I'd like to find some milder color paper, but I don't know how to ask for it.

We're in the store and I'm trying to concoct the right phrasing in my head. Then I look at Sara. She's holding my hand looking around, patiently waiting. I have an idea. I kneel down and whisper:

"Hey, how would you ask for colored paper in Croatian?" She pauses, thinks a bit and says,

"Daddy, come here. I'll whisper it to you." I lean in and she tells me.

"Gdje Vam je obojani papir?"

She put Vam in there, I think, *I would have never thought of that. Vam* is the Croatian pronoun for "you all," and the formal version of you. Like the royal we, but you know, with you.

I ask the seller and she leads us to a whole variety of colored paper. *Success!* I look at my daughter, beaming with pride. Five years old and my bilingual little decoder. It's like having my own, child version of C3PO walking around with me. Programmed for etiquette and protocol, and… sometimes tantrums.

Here we are, father and daughter walking down the sidewalk with a bag of paper from the "People's Papers," heading back to our rented apartment. Nearly a decade before and I had no idea where Zagreb or Croatia was. I couldn't ever imagine living here. But then I met my wife on a cold winter's night in Oklahoma. And here we were, a binational, bilingual family living in a place I once thought was Russia.

I look at this kid next to me and remember how she had once just been an abstract idea, *Daughter,* just like Croatia had once been an abstract idea, *Somewhere*. However, in the present both are now real. Both are now named and with dimension. Both are now the mass around which my life orbits.

CHAPTER I

It takes a cyber village to feel at home

It was a dreary, drizzling January evening in Zagreb. I stopped at a kiosk on Vukovarska to buy Sara a kids' magazine. She'd gone to the dentist or had been to the doctor, or something, I forget, and I'd promised to get her a magazine for being brave. Zagreb's kiosks host a large number of kids magazines, all with names like: *Barbie weekly*, *Princess monthly*, *Disney Princess Pets*, and *My Little Pony Digest*.

Each one comes wrapped in cellophane with a toy inside. I opted for the My Little Pony magazine because it looked like it came with the best gift, which was really the whole point of getting a kid's magazine since Sara couldn't yet read. And if I read it to her it would be in such garbled Croatian that she could only take so much. Half a sentence in and she'd say, "Daddy... Get Mama." We'd been there before.

As I handed the magazine up to the saleswoman, she sort of gave me a strange smile, something knowing, but not quite a full smirk. And I thought, *yeah it's funny that a grown man is buying a My Little Pony magazine. Ha-ha.* But then, she asked if I was Cody. Not Dr. Brown, not Mr.

Brown, not Mr. Cody, certainly not Dr. Cody, but just plain old Cody. Startled, I mumbled out a *jesam* (I am) and watched her smile break into a full grin.

"*Vaš blog je super*" she replied (Your blog is super). *Whaaa?* A random stranger in a random kiosk reads my blog? And says it's "super?"

This is success. I had made it. I was on a first name basis with… the world!

I'd come a long way from being a friendless foreigner in Croatia. A few years ago, I'd moved to Croatia. After a period of um… adjustment, we (my wife and I) had decided to try and live here. I'd decided that Croatia could be home. And now, well, I was learning that that's easier said than done. But, here I was getting recognized by the lady working in the kiosk. I mean, how cool is that? Clearly, I think it's pretty cool, and unexpected, like really unexpected. I thanked her, smiled, thanked her again and kept smiling.

Right, so I write a blog and I wrote a book, called *Chasing a Croatian Girl*. And the book you are currently holding in your hands, or reading on a screen, is the sequel to that book. So here we are again. This book is called *Croatia Strikes Back* because I'm a *Star Wars* fan and just like the film with a similar title was the second movie in the original *Star Wars* trilogy, this is my second book. But, the title also refers to how difficult it can be to try and carve out a life here, and not just for a foreigner like me, but for your normal, everyday Croatians too. In the first book I decided to live in Croatia, and this books deals with the reality of that decision. But don't worry, I mean it's not THAT bad.

The biggest challenge to life in Croatia is hope. That's what this book is about, because the main thing I've learned from living in Croatia, from teaching hundreds of students at the university, from becoming a member of a Croatian family, from forming Croatian friendships, is that having hope in Croatia is hard. It's as if there is some vague force of darkness trying to eclipse even the thinnest rays of optimism. And the puzzling thing is that while Croatia is the most beautiful, safest, nicest place I've ever lived in, and the people have welcomed me in a way that I don't feel any immigrant would receive in the US (or elsewhere in Europe), Croatia can also feel more hopeless than any of the other places I've lived in, especially compared to the United States. And while hope in Croatia is hard, its absence is offset by the strong personal relationships that tie individuals to the broader society. In Croatia it can be hopeless, but you never feel alone. In America, hope is abundant, but so too, is loneliness.

But first let's back up a bit and let me briefly explain my blog. It began as a blog about Croatian tax policy, which, unsurprisingly, no one read. So, then I turned it into a blog about the cultural differences between Croatia and America. I wrote about things that I was trying to understand like Croatians' fear of moving air and drafts, how pleasant the indifferent, sometimes negligent, customer service in Croatia's cafes and restaurants can be, especially compared to the faux-polite-tip-seeking interruptions in American restaurants, and of course my mother-in-law, punica. Who, by the way, was now enjoying her own sort of notoriety, at times even being referred to as, THE punica. Begun in November 2012, by February 2013 it was... a thing. One website named it the best blog about

Croatia I was featured in a few newspapers and news websites.

Even, then, three-and-a-half-year-old Sara knew about it, and that was saying something because at the age of three how can your toddler even hope to know what a blog is. It's not like she could use the computer or read. I figured this out one day when I was in the bathroom, trying to clean up a mess. The drain had backed up again, sending a slew of grey, gurgling sludge gushing forth, covering the tile floor in a few... *centimeters* (eh, eh... I'm learning) of water. I stood in the middle of it, barefoot with my pants rolled up to my knees, gingerly picking up a bunch of soaked towels and tossing them into the shower. Sara looked on with fascination from the hallway, anticipating when I would pop off the lid of the drain and try to fix the problem. She liked that kinda stuff.

Sloshing towards the drain I yelled to Vana, "If I can't fix it this time we'll have to call a plumber."

Then Sara piped up, "Yeah," she added. "Because you're not a real plumber." I looked at her. "You just have a blog."

By the time I was recognized at that kiosk, I'd even been on TV. And yes, I had been recognized a few times on the street, mostly in the more popular places in Zagreb, never in a place so random as a kiosk. But, usually I'm recognized after half an hour of conversation with a friend of a friend who suddenly stops and says, "Oh you're *that* American." Yeah, I guess, I'm *that* American.

And being *that* American is a whole lot better than just being *an* American. My Croatian life can basically be divided into two parts, before the blog and after the blog. As you may know, moving to another country can be an incredibly alienating experience. All of my friends and family were back in the US, and though I hadn't lost complete contact with them, our lives began to diverge in so many ways that the core commonality of our friendship began to break and crumble under the stress. They couldn't relate to what I was doing in my life (*Two hours? Drinking one coffee? Whaaaat?*) and I increasingly forgot what it was like to do whatever it was they were doing in theirs (*Making... money?*). The gift of social networking and cyber-life did not extend to the spontaneity and familiarity found in true friendships.

And while everything was new to me in Croatia, the lack of familiarity with anyone outside of my immediate family, was increasingly isolating. We weren't on vacation. This wasn't a backpacking trip designed to give us "new experiences." Our move was supposed to be for good. We'd committed our lives to living in Croatia, but at the back of my mind there was a persistent voice challenging the permanence of this endeavor with a consistent chorus of doubt, a refrain that repeatedly reminded me that Croatia was not my home.

Those first two years were subsumed with uncertainty: could I really build a life here? Could I find steady work? Everyone said that it was all but impossible for a foreigner. Could I conform? Would I be able to ever feel like anything other than an outsider?

Just around this time someone appropriately began spray painting a stencil of Bear Grylls, the host of the show *Man vs Wild* or *Ultimate Survival,* all over Zagreb's city center. Everywhere I walked I saw fucking Bear Grylls, peeking from Zagreb's pock-marked facades. Below his stenciled face was the question: "How long could you survive in Croatia?"

I felt like he was directly asking me. *Seriously, universe? Here in my moment of doubt the heavens conspire to graffiti all over Zagreb the question I keep asking myself?* I mean really, this was some kind of karmic, cosmic coincidence shit. Again and again the question popped up, plaguing my periphery like the rhythmic passing of a train: "How long?" "How long?" "How long?" And with each step I worried, because I didn't know.

One day, during Zagreb's amber autumn, when the leaves had yellowed and the chestnuts had begun dropping all across the sidewalks, I had the realization of just how friendless I was. The only two people I ever called on my phone were Vana and punica? *Oh shit*. OK, calling your wife that often... well alright, that's kinda nice. But, your mother-in-law? *Gah!* I mean this is like the premise for a sitcom.

Slavic Mother-in-law and American Son!

What was perhaps even worse was that everyday I was gathering enough humorous material for an *actual* sitcom, and yet I had no one to share it with. And having no one to laugh at your jokes is the worst. It's the sad clown level of sadness.

Then the blog happened, and soon I had a whole lot of people laughing at my jokes. While Likes on Facebook and comments on Blogger couldn't really replace real friendship, they did allow me to feel accepted. Every writer wants an audience, and not only did I get one, I got one that chatted back with me. As I wrote about all the crazy cultural misunderstandings I was experiencing, I realized that I wasn't alone.

Bear and his soul stirring rhetorical question

In fact, a lot of Croatians who are married to foreigners had experienced the same awkward, frustrating, and at times hilarious situations I had. And a lot of Croatians who immigrated to the US or elsewhere like Australia, were trying to explain their culture to a bunch of bewildered locals. People began commenting on the blog, sharing it and writing messages, thanking me for explaining what… well… for a long time they thought was unexplainable.

Writing the blog was like a kind of therapy, a process of reconciling my culture and my mind with Croatian culture and our life here. But, posting the blog, getting all the audience feedback and comments, became like a group therapy session for foreigners and Croatians alike.

It is the best form of validation for a stranger in a strange land, and those times where I still feel the crushing distance from my old friends and my ever aging family, when I wake up thinking, *my God, what have I done!?!* Or when I bemoan the fact that I'm not a *real* plumber, especially when that drain keeps backing up, I find some solace in thinking *well, at least I've got a blog* and most importantly, *those who read it.*

CHAPTER 2

Boredom, the great breeding ground of friendship

Sliding into adulthood can be a lonely experience. Most of my older, life-long friends are scattered around the continental US. In America, once you go off to college your friends fall into three categories, those who stay behind, those who leave and come back, and those who never return (OK, fine, yes on holidays, but you know what I mean). My closest friends belong to the last category. We spread out from Oklahoma like seeds dispersed by the wind, laying down roots on the West Coast, the East Coast, and a few places in the middle.

And then there's me, here in Croatia.

That brings us to the second thing that's a lonely experience, growing up *and* moving to a foreign country. As much as the blog's emerging cyber-self-help group helped me feel less isolated, I still lacked *real* friends. Not only was I away from my friends, but gone was that kind of subliminal familiarity that helps define home. That knowledge that's more like instinct, where knowing how to get somewhere is like breathing, and knowing how to behave around someone you've known for ages is like feeling your own heartbeat, you barely notice it at all. I missed that intimate knowledge. At the beginning it was hard to believe that I could ever become that familiar with my new, foreign surroundings.

Add to this the time constraints wrought by work and parenthood, and well I just didn't think I'd ever find the time for friends. I've met a lot of great people, and had coffee with a lot of great people (which in Croatia is the true prelude to friendship), yet the time needed to invest in a new relationship, let alone to understand a new culture, seemed to always be lacking.

Or so I thought...

In the warmer months, between April and November, we used to always stop at the park near Sara's preschool. Sara would run around and play, and as she grew older I didn't need to stand right next to her while she climbed on the bars of the jungle-gym that's shaped like a train. I'd often spy a nearby bench and... just sit.

Now, back then, the park had already been a landscape of cross culture exchange. At the beginning when we were new, Sara and I stood out like... a couple of Americans in a park in Croatia. Since I spoke English to her and she spoke English to me, it was always obvious that we were from out of town. Sara was technically from Split (the city referred to by my wife, punica and all its residents as "the most beautiful place in the world"). Upon hearing us talk, the other parents would just give us an inquisitive glance; however, to the other, older kids, it was like the circus had come into town. Some would whisper in some kind of bewildered awe that we were speaking English (and this just goes to show how polyglot Croatians are from an early age, a five year-old can recognize and name a foreign language heard on the playground). Some of the kids would often ask me to say something in English, while other kids would sort of confront me about it.

"Why are you speaking English?" One six or seven year-old demanded to know in Croatian. "This is Croatia!"

"I'm speaking English, because I'm an American," I replied in some *kind* of Croatian.

"Liar! You're not American, you're speaking Croatian." *Whoa... what? My Croatian is good enough for me to not be American in the eyes of a kid? Hmm, life's just full of surprises.*

"Of course," I said, still "speaking" Croatian. "I live in Croatia. I need to speak Croatian."

This was too much, even for me, I was becoming lost in my own logic. If I needed to speak Croatian in Croatia, why had I just been speaking English with Sara? The kid and I were locked in a stalemate. We just kind of looked at each other, unsure of where things should go from there. Then from the bars on the already mentioned, nearby jungle-gym-train, four-year-old Sara stepped in.

"Hey boy (dečko)," she hollered. "I speak four languages! Splitski, Croatian, American and English."

The kid looked at Sara, and then at me. What could I say, she was right... err... sort of. I gave the kid a shrug. He paused for a heartbeat, as if deciding that none of this was worth it. Then he ran off, shaking his head as if the whole thing was just a confusing waste of time. I looked over at Sara, smiling, and she just went on climbing.

Aside from encounters like this, sitting on the bench, in the park, day in and day out, back in the beginning, was... pretty... boring. Thank God! Because, as I learned, there is no better way to make a friend than to find another bored parent. It's like the grownup equivalent to school. You have to be there, you're bored, hell, might as well talk to someone, maybe make a friend.

Now, if the situation was reversed, and I was a foreigner living in Oklahoma, I don't know if this would have happened. For parents of young children, a Zagreb park acts like the center of the universe. Since few of us have yards to play in, all the kids play at the park with the parents hanging around. In the US, during my childhood when I went out to play it was usually with the other neighborhood kids in their yard or our yard. Our parents never came along with us. I can't ever really recall my parents being friends with the parents of my friends. They knew each other, sure, but it doesn't seem like they were ever really friends, especially not in the Croatian sense of the word "friend."

No, if the situation were reversed, I fear that no American or Croatian would ever find themselves bored in the same spot, long enough and regularly enough to become friends.

One day Sara is playing with a girl she's been playing with quite regularly. Slowly I realize that this girl, Nora, is in her group at preschool. I glance around and there's her dad standing nearby looking as bored as I am. Sara and her friend, Nora, come up and say something to us both. Sara in English, Nora in Croatian. After I respond, Nora's father, Mirko, asks me,

"Where are you from?" Only in Croatian. Now this is always a difficult question. If I answer "America" that might be too obvious, like "duh". If I say "Oklahoma" then that might be too vague. This guy looks like he'd be able to tell I'm American, so I opt for a compromise.

"Oklahoma, it's near Texas." And then we keep talking... in Croatian. I ask him what he does and he says he's a pilot. Eventually, and honestly I'm not sure how we get to this point, but we end up in a detailed discussion concerning the exorbitant costs of the US Air force's F-35 stealth fighter. And while the conversation begins in Croatian and continues in Croatian for a bit, this guy can see when I'm out of my depth. And guess what? Discussing advanced aviation technology in Croatia means I'm out of my depth. He switches to a fluent, though accented English. And no, I can't talk about football. No, I can't talk about cars. No, I can't talk about UFC, but what I can talk about, and at length, is bloated, wasteful bureaucratic defense spending! And fortunately, so could Mirko.

The next day it's the same thing, the day after that, and the next, until all the days blur into routine and I've found something similar to the familiarity of home that I'd missed so much. And before we know it, our daughters are best friends and we're hanging out in the park, staying when we pick the kids up at each other's houses, and even getting coffee or a beer by ourselves in the local cafe.

And then it happens again with another one of Sara's friends, Sonja and her parents Adrian and Marta. Each time we go to pick Sara up from their place, we end up staying an hour, two hours, drinking a beer or two, eating all their chips, talking, and having a good time. One of the great things about this couple are the stories they have about a vacation they took to America, in 1986! They tell me about their impressions and what impressed them... like air conditioning in a car! Or how Adrian searched all over the

Smithsonian Museum in Washington DC, looking for a toilet because all he saw were signs for the "restroom" (in Croatia and the rest of Europe it's the WC, short for Water Closet) and he thought, *Well, it's a big museum, I guess they need rooms to rest.*

As time goes on and the friendships between our kids grow, the park becomes not just their meeting point, but ours as well. Dormant in the winter, muddy and gray with lifeless benches and branches, each spring the park becomes the living center of our world, until the summer comes and everyone heads to the coast. And when I say "park" for the parents what I really mean is the wooden deck of the cafe near the park. Each afternoon we meet and sit, drinking coffee and often beer, while our kids run around and play.

It feels like half the neighborhood is here. And if someone isn't sitting outside the cafe, then they are walking by. I see our older upstairs neighbor stroll pass, I see the familiar faces of the preschool parents. I sit and feel like we are all part of a community.

As a foreigner, or maybe by this point I'm an immigrant, there is always a doubt about belonging that rests at the back of your mind. You wonder if you'll ever truly move from the outside in (and sure, the blog was helping in this transition, but what about in the real world?). As a parent you wonder if your kid will ever be fully integrated and accepted. But before you know it, we parents, Vana, Mirko and Vesna, Adrian and Marta, Krešo and a few others, have a little society, a circle of friends familiar enough that formality fades, familiar enough that I forget not only where I am, but more, importantly, where I'm not.

CHAPTER 3

Flying Kid Kicks at Midnight

After the blog became popular, I'd sometimes meet people who had read it and we would talk about cultural differences between Americans and Croatians. And often times, I would talk about whatever "difference" was dominating my domestic life at the time. One day, I met a woman on a bench while Sara was playing at the park and I let that conversation go to some surprising places. The woman said she'd read and enjoyed my blog, but then she asked me, "Do you really think Croatians and Americans are that different?"

"Oh yeah." I replied. "One thing that really sticks out is just different styles in parenting."

"Like what?" she asked.

"Well, think of bedtime or just sleeping. Like, in the US, training your kid to sleep alone and on cue is one of the first things parents do. From friends and family, it's like a badge of how good a parent you are. Is your little Ben sleeping through the night, yet? The "yet" is really important. Oh yeah, he's been sleeping through since he was 8 weeks old, alone. What about little Jane? Oh, she was practically born sleeping at night, and alone."

"And how is it here, with you all?"

I looked at this person I barely knew, and yet to whom I was about to reveal the details of my domestic situation. I paused for a second or two, considering how to answer this question. How should I explain how vastly different it is between here and there. How could I conjure the infinite distance between how my sister and her friends raise their kids in America's capital, Washington DC, and how Vana, Sara and I live? Finally I replied, "I sleep in a child's bed with a poster of a Disney princess hung up over it."

After that she didn't really know what to say, and who would? She just looked at me a bit, the confusion as apparent on her face as the summer sun, cutting through the leaves.

"It's a long story," I replied.

One spring afternoon we rearranged the bedroom. For the last two years, since we'd moved into this apartment we'd all slept in the only bedroom with a big bed pushed against a small twin bed. That way there was enough room for me, Vana and baby Sara. However, Sara was now three, it was time for her to begin sleeping in her own bed, but just across the room from our bed. Vana bought some colorful princess themed bedsheets from the movie *Tangled*. Sara was very into *Tangled* (much more than *Frozen,* and *Tangled* is a much better movie). In order to help ease the process we made a big deal about how *awesome* and *beautiful* the bedsheets were, and how great it was that Sara would be sleeping in her own bed! Like some ominous foreshadowing, I exclaimed with a little too much enthusiasm,

"Man, I wish I could sleep with such awesome sheets!" Sara seemed excited and into it.

We separated her bed from our bed, it was like a sapling hewed from the parent tree. We vacuumed up all the dust that had gathered over the years behind the beds. We pushed Sara's bed into a cleared corner of the bedroom. We put a little pink rug in front of her bed. I clipped out a poster of Rapunzel from one of the princess magazines sold at the kiosks and let Sara hang it up over her new bed. *This is really happening!* I thought. *Tonight my wife and I will sleep in the same bed, alone! I'll have space!*

Ever since she was born, Sara had slept with us. The bed used to be so big that she would sometimes have to crawl all the way over to me from the other side. But now, she just had to stretch her foot out a bit, and I was abruptly awoken with a swift kick in the small of my back: *Oof! What the... Oh, it's just my kid kicking me at 3 AM.* Sara was all snuggles with Vana, I was all feet and her feet were like mindless octopus tentacles, they moved and writhed everywhere. There was no pattern to their madness. I'd get a kick in the square of my back, shift over, fall asleep and wake up with her foot on my face. I'd gently try to bend her leg or turn her around. I'd fall back asleep, only to get one foot in my neck and another one on the top of my head. I'd wake up in disbelief and look quizzically at my sleeping daughter and wife.

This has to be a joke, right? I mean they both have to be in on this, pretending to be asleep, laughing at how Sara's feet keep flying in dad's face. I bet they plan it each night, the jerks. I imagined them drawing intricate diagrams about where and when Sara should place her feet, triangulating the time and places that promised to provide optimum annoyance.

I'd look closely at them in the wee light, searching for the tell-tale smile of someone feigning sleep. But no, she and Vana were sleeping like logs. I'd survey the situation. It was always hopeless. There was no way I could conceivably find any comfortable space in the bed. *Ah screw it,* I'd think. *It's 5 AM, I might as well just get up and write.* And now, you know what led me to be a writer.

Well not anymore! Sure. I was ready to sacrifice my art for a night of sound sleeping without any kid feet flying in my face.

Fast forward a few months and as I drift off to sleep, I look at the askew Rapunzel poster adhered to the wall with strips of cello-tape that look like smudgy bandages. Beneath her wide eyes and amid the tangles of her long magic hair, Rapunzel is smiling. In the half-light of the nighttime room, I'm pretty sure she's mocking me. I have the sense she's smirking, laughing inwardly at how my wife and daughter sleep cuddled together comfortably on the bigger, better bed just across the room, and how I'm in a bed that's too short, too narrow, and draped with princess themed bedsheets. *How did this happen?*

Yep, back when I dreamed of one day of being a writer in Europe, this is just how I imagined I would go to sleep each night when I was married and 35 years old.

By now I've learned we aren't the only family with this issue. Most of our friends also sleep with their kids in their bed. Over coffee one day with Mirko I complain about the size of our apartment.

"We need more room. I'd like Sara to have her own room," I say. Mirko looks at me, shaking his head. He'd recently moved into a larger apartment.

"Trust me, you don't need a bigger apartment. You just need a bigger bed."

Even after we made Sara's bed she kept getting up and climbing in with us, and I'd get kicked again. And this time without the spatial benefit her bed used to bring to our sleeping arrangement. Her bed was over there, sitting empty and useless. Then I went on a trip to the US for three weeks and while I was gone, she and Vana shared the big bed. Then she got sick and stayed in the bed for a few more days and… my sleeping in Sara's bed just became an act of convenience.

And in Croatia, at least within my parenting cohort, we lay down with our kids until they fall asleep. I tried to stop doing this, to have Sara learn to fall asleep on her own, but she was too used to someone being with her. When I would leave she told me she was too scared.

"Scared of what?" I asked, expecting something like ghosts, witches or vampires. This is the Balkans after all.

"A Crocodile," she replied. Her eyes wide with genuine worry.

"A Crocodile?" I really didn't expect that. *Well, good* I thought, *that's easy to fix*. I decided to use logic.

"Sweetie, are there crocodiles in Croatia?"

"At the zoo."

"That's right, only at the zoo. It's not like Egypt or other countries where crocodiles live in the wild. And walk around. So, you have nothing to worry about. The only crocodile in the country is at the zoo."

She nodded, but didn't look convinced.

"Are you still scared?"

She nodded again.

"Alright look. It's impossible for a crocodile to get into our bedroom. I mean, he would have to first break out of the zoo, then get to our neighborhood, which would take a really long time because he can't walk that fast and there is no way to swim here. Then, he would need to find a ladder, use that ladder to climb up to our apartment, get someone to open the window, and then slip into the apartment without us knowing, hide, and only come out when I leave the room and turn off the light. Do you really think a crocodile could do all that?"

Sara looked at me, her eyes wider. Looked at the window. Looked back at me.

"Yes," she said as if it was the most obvious thing in the world. In fact I'd just laid out the way in which *it could be done*.

So, it turned out it was also easier for Vana and myself to put Sara to sleep in our bed, but then we would fall asleep too. I would get up later and move to Sara's bed. It was easier than falling asleep together, crammed on a small kid's bed. And so...

Sleeping alone not only saves me from kid kicks in the middle of the night, but it also helps with my and Vana's biggest and greatest cultural disagreement. You know, that one about the health effects of moving air.

Ah, my old nemesis Dr. Propuh, we meet again.

In Croatia *propuh* is the Joker to my Batman, the Lex Luthor to my Superman, the Pepsi to my Coke, the Rolling Stones to my Beatles, the Galactic Empire to my Rebel Alliance.

Let me familiarize you with the clash of cultures surrounding the phenomenon of *propuh*. *Propuh* is the word for the draft, moving air in an enclosed space. In America this is pleasant. In Croatia, it is considered deadly! Propuh is thought to be the cause of all kinds of ailments, the most deadly and insidious of which is inflammation of the brain (by the way, this was a phrase I had never heard until I got involved with a Croatian). How *propuh* works is not really known. It's mysterious. Nevertheless I've had all kinds of people try to explain why the health effects of *propuh* are a real concern through various theories, including a student presentation that linked the draft's effects to Newton's 2nd law of thermodynamics. Yet, I remain stubbornly unconvinced. No matter how much my relatives, neighbors, friends, strangers and students insist that *propuh* is dangerous, by some miracle, Americans are immune to the damaging effects of *propuh*.

What this means is that when it's hot, I want to open the window or turn on the fan in order to cool down. My Croatian family looks at this as if I'm trying to commit suicide. Now for people like my punica, *propuh* is not a joke. It's serious, deadly serious.

At first I had to argue with punica when I wanted to turn the fan on at night when the ambient temperature was around 28 degrees celsius. Eventually, she came around and like Pontius Pilate washed her hands of responsibility, saying "Well, if you want to kill yourself, that's fine, but I tried to warn you!"

Now what does all this have to to with my sleeping in a too-small-bed under a Rapunzel poster? Well, Sara's arrival into our lives changed the whole debate. To have a fan blowing at a bed with a child in it!?! That's tantamount to child abuse, or worse: attempted murder.

In the eyes of my family I went from someone who doesn't want to sleep in a tangle of sweaty sheets to a villain of mythic Greek proportions, a villain right out of some great tragedy ready to commit matricide and prolicide (the act of killing one's offspring) just so I could keep cool in the middle of the night. I could already hear the old ladies discuss it on the bench in front of our apartment. *Cody was tired of sweating through the night, so he turned a fan on his whole family.* Heads shake, *Tragic*.

Well, punica and Vana weren't having it. Fans blowing on the bed while Sara slept within: strictly forbidden. In fact it was *Verbotten!* That's at the German language level of forbidden. And you don't want to mess with that. And I was pretty sure that if I pushed this, insisting on the harmlessness of moving air during a hot summer night with Sara's safety under question... well then Vana might be the one committing some matricide and my mother-in-law would most certainly indulge in some son-in-law-i-cide. And at trial they'd be acquitted because everyone in Croatia knows, *propuh* is deadly.

The flying kid kicks pushed me out of the bed, but I continue to sleep alone because of *propuh*.

So, I go to sleep looking at the Rapunzel poster, only this time a corner flaps gently in the breeze of the oscillating fan. It's a hot night, the windows are open, the air is still. As I drift off to sleep I feel a bit like an outsider, a stranger in my own home, forced by circumstance (single bedroom apartment, small bed, Sara kicks, and *propuh*) into a slumbering exile.

CHAPTER 4

Punica's house is wherever punica is

Life at home wasn't just complicated by the fact that I was sleeping alone in a child-sized bed, and enjoying it. It was also complicated by the monthly incursions of my mother-in-law into our apartment. As I mentioned in the last chapter, punica would disapprove if I slept in a bed with a fan blowing on me and Sara... and you might be asking, um... you don't live with your punica so how would she know? And I'd respond by saying... you, dear reader must not be Croatian. Punica knows! SHE ALWAYS KNOWS!

Each time Punica came to our apartment, which was monthly and usually for two weeks, she kind of took over. In my mind it was like a foreign occupation led by a septuagenarian tsar. What had been my "little America" was transformed over night into the "REPUBLIC OF PUNICA."

When I was growing up, my grandparents often came and stayed with us. During their stay my grandmother never cooked lunch or dinner, she never did the household laundry, she never cleaned. And this was not considered bad, nor did it violate some kind of grandma social contract. It was considered perfectly normal. If my grandparents were visiting on holidays, she might've helped make one of the side dishes or helped set the table. My parents' house was my parents' house, and my grandparents' house was my grandparents' house. There was a clear and distinct border between these two worlds. This included how my mother and step-father dealt with my sister and me. I cannot recall my grandmother or grandfather ever telling my parents how they should treat me. I'm sure there were times when they wanted to, or when they later gave some advice, but this was never done in front of me. Both sides honored each other's primacy in their respected domains.

Then there is our situation in Croatia. Every time punica comes up to Zagreb I catch her casting a disdainful glare at the untidiness of our apartment. Sure, the dishes are all clean, the table is clear, the living room freshly vacuumed, Vana has made sure to scrub everything, and I've even set a nice candle center piece in the middle of the table, but I've also neglected an errant sock under the corner of the couch and few malinger bread crumbs on one of the placemats. It's all the evidence she needs to know that we, Vana and I, are incapable of properly maintaining a household, and that we *desperately* need her to begin cleaning.

Whenever my mother-in-law comes to stay with us, it is the exact opposite of how my grandma used to come and stay with my family. Punica constantly cooks and cleans. At first, it's kind of nice. It's like having a servant come and stay with you for two weeks. Except of course that during her work this servant condescends to you about why she has to do all these things. Reason, because she believes you are horrible at doing them yourself.

In my last book I refer to punica as a drug dealer because by doing everything around the house she made us dependent on her. By placing prohibitions on my wife or me doing the cooking when she was around, we grew accustomed to her doing all the cooking. When she was gone we ate the precooked meals she'd placed in the freezer. When those were gone, we ordered pizza or takeout. Sometimes we cooked, but it was just a stop gap measure, a half-hearted act to fill our bellies until the real deal returned. In short, like a couple of junkies, we were addicted to punica. However, after four years of this, I desperately wanted to break the habit.

But, I love my mother-in-law. It's not that I don't want her to come to Zagreb, I just want her to be a bit more like my American grandma and respect my space.

My punica is a stout, sturdy, woman in her mid 70s. If I picture her, I see her wearing an apron, carrying a wooden spoon and mumbling to herself about what needs done and when she needs to do it. She is an industrious worker, cooking and cleaning for the whole family whenever she's around. Her apartment is kept in immaculate shape. There is barely any dust anywhere (even under the beds!) And she seems to be motivated by the single-minded concern of making sure my daughter, myself, and her daughter are well fed and warm (even when there is no need because it's hot outside). It's pretty wonderful when you think about it.

And then when you stop thinking about it, but begin living it, it's a bit less than wonderful… Croatia's mother-in-laws always and forever see their children as CHILDREN! My punica will call and ask things about my daughter like: Did Sara eat? Is it cold? Is Sara dressed warm enough? She'll call my wife and ask her: Did you eat? Is it cold? Are you dressed warm enough? Did Sara eat? Is she dressed warm enough?

The older generation in Croatia seems to believe that in their absence, we are all children. And not just children, but like 4-year-olds. And it bothers me. It's like my adulthood is on trial. I imagine I'm in court, standing before a jury of 12 grey-haired grandmas trying to prove my competence as a person, a father, a husband… an adult.

"Your Honor, let the record show," I say before the court. "I have moved to a foreign country. I've completed advanced levels of education. Elsewhere in the country people actually call me *doctor*. I am married. I have sired and raised a daughter and yet, I am still treated as if I am a child, nay, an idiot, an idiot child, in my own home." I can see the grey-haired jury grumbling, wringing their hands in their aprons, adjusting their bifocals, and menacingly, sharpening their wooden spoons.

Back in the real world, punica undermines my case by saying things like, "You are smart, that's clear, but I, I have experience!" The tension made by the incongruence of our idiosyncrasies builds with each visit.

Punica comes to Zagreb by bus. As usual, I pick her up from the bus station and bring her back to our apartment. She's tired, it's a long trip for a… um… not young woman. I lug her suitcase up the stairs and set it down in our apartment's hallway. Each time I do this I feel as if I'm missing some bit of ceremony to my punica's arrival. The suitcase, the well-worn rug, the hugs to Vana and Sara all have the feel and rhythm of a ritual, only I lack the devotion needed to make this act sacred.

Even while in the middle of this single action I want something to let me know now, that later this moment will mean more than it presently does. I want to comprehend that these moments, though routine, are fleeting and that soon, too soon, my punica will be too old to make the regular trek from Split to Zagreb. And I want to understand amid this simple, fleeting action that in the near future I will look back on my mother-in-law's arrivals with regret. I want to know now that I will regret not having had more patience, that I'll regret not letting her constant comments on everything fade harmlessly into the background like the white noise of the rushing traffic. But such insight is elusive in the present. So, I set her suitcase down on the well-worn rug in the hallway, missing the appreciation of this act. I only know that I'm already sorry we aren't going to get along.

Punica comes in like a tornado, only instead of creating chaos, she creates order, but it's a new order, one I'm never consulted about in my own apartment. She rearranges things according to her whims and wishes. I open drawers and cabinets only to find their contents have migrated to other cabinets and drawers. The totality of her reign is so complete that it has a lasting legacy. Later, when we need to know if we have a certain ingredient for dinner or in the event we can't find something, we have to call her up and ask her. And she's five hours away, back in Split.

The next time she comes up to Zagreb we talk about it and I try to explain how her ways are completely at odds with how I was raised. She is not moved. She's a bit dismissive and is basically under the impression that I live in Croatia now, so it's my job to adapt to my new environment. Which is fair, except that we are in *my* apartment and thus she could try to accommodate *my* culture. It's no use. We are at an impasse, locked in a dispute over territory, autonomy and sovereignty. We can't agree on the extent to which either one of us has the right to our own culture, customs and self-determination.

Then one day my punica explains to me that this is just how it is. Period. The earth orbits the sun, the tide comes in, the tide goes out, and Croatian mothers and grandmothers worry about the well-being of their kids *forever*. Even her own mother, punica explains, used to worry about her and comment on everything. She told me that when her mother was 90 years old she would stop my punica as she left to go to the market and say, "Be careful when you cross the street, I heard an accident yesterday at the intersection."

Inwardly I fall over, drop to the floor with my hand on my head thinking: *Oh man, this is never going to end*. But then I also realize that yes, it. is. *never*. going. to. end. If at 90 someone can see her 60 something year-old daughter as a child, then there was no way I can get my mid 70s punica to see me as an adult, no matter how many books I write or doctorates I attain. I mean, I'm *only* 35. If anything I must look even more like a child since I do everything the opposite of what she would do, which from her view must look like I am always doing EVERYTHING wrong. In her mind, I'm sure, I really am a child. I know it. I see how she looks at me with a hard determination, lamenting how much harder she has to work whenever I'm involved. *Oh lord, why did you have to send an imbecile American? Why couldn't Vana have married a real Croatian, better yet a Dalmatian? Like Ante, Stipe or Mate!*

The more I look at it from her perspective that more I see that I'm the problem. She is really just trying to help. I know this because she regularly says things to me like,

"I'm really just trying to help."

Yet, it is still strange to have someone come over and then critique everything I do in my own house. Punica says things like: Don't lay your clothes over this chair. Oh you're spending money. Don't give Sara a *burek*, giver her a *bublica*. I couldn't help taking umbrage to this steady stream of critique. I somehow heard the words *idiot* and *dumb-ass* before each of my punica's utterances.

She might say, "Oh you're spending money." And what I hear is, "Hey *idiot*, you're spending money on stupid things!"

On the other hand, to punica, everything she says I'm sure sounds like nice, useful, sought-after advice. She probably thinks she sounds something like this,

"Oh, dear son-in-law, you might not be aware of this, since you are young and... an inexperienced foreigner, but it is not always the best idea to spend money on things that are not essential. If you don't have any money, how will you buy soup?"

She isn't trying to be insulting by pointing out that everything I do seems wrong, she is *trying* to be *helpful*.

What can I do? Culture is the sum of all our learned behavior, I can't just become someone else as much as I'd like to. I can't just unlearn who I am and where I came from, and neither can punica.

And this goes on until one summer Vana and I go on something called the *Boat of Culture*. We sail around to different Adriatic islands giving readings and spoken word performances each night. It's a great time. Sara stays with punica in Split, giving Vana and me some time to ourselves. Everyday we have breakfast and lunch on the boat, prepared for us by the cook and served by the waiter in the galley. We literally don't have to do anything, and we very much have nothing to do. It's wonderful. At one point, though, I jokingly say to Vana, with a beer in my hand, looking out over the sea's blue horizon,

"What do you think punica would do if she were on this boat?"

"If Sara was with us, she'd probably want to help with lunch," Vana replies. I can't imagine punica ever being this idle, at least not when her kids or grandkids are around. And then, like a bolt of lightning I get it. I understand. The clouds have parted. A dove comes flying out of the storm. I want to stand up and say "*Hallelujah!* I have seen the light! Oh Lawd! I have seen the light!"

I realize that punica can't help it. There is a lesson here, and that lesson is: everywhere is potentially your punica's house. To my mother-in-law there is no physical, social, or mental boundary between her place and our place. She is our mother, and thus wherever we are that she is, we are in her house.

This should be a slogan in a handbook given to all foreign-born husbands in Croatia: *Wherever your punica is, even when she's in your house, that's her house. It's all her house. Sit down and eat.*

So now I've learned that whenever punica comes to Zagreb, my house is no longer my house. It's her house and I'm just a guest. We're getting along fine.

CHAPTER 5

The Missing Chapter

Here was where the chapter I'd written about working at Croatian Radio Television (HRT) and The Voice of Croatia was supposed to go, but on the advice of several friends, family, and a lawyer, I decided to omit it, because Croatia has very strong libel laws. America doesn't. That's why I can call US President Trump a liar with tiny hands. For some reason in the US, powerful people and institutions seem to rarely sue other people for things they say about them. I mean in the US, I can say Barack Obama doesn't understand regular Americans because he is too much of a Kenyan marxist. Actually, I didn't say that, but former Speaker of the House of Representatives, Newt Gingrich did. And no one sued him. In the US, I could stand on stage next to George W. Bush when he was President and say "I believe that the government that governs best is a government that governs least, and by these standards we have set up a fabulous government in Iraq." Because, that's exactly what Stephen Colbert did at the 2006 White House Correspondents' Dinner. And look, he later got the Late Show from David Letterman. If there is one thing

Americans know how to do, it's take a joke (or vote for one, apparently).

Now, in the now "missing" chapter I don't think I wrote anything mean-spirited about HRT. Rather, and this is what comedy is all about, I wrote about things that everyone knows are true. To quote someone whose name I forgot, "Humor is not about being comical, it's about being accurate." So, I wrote, in my opinion some "accurate" things about Croatia's national broadcaster and the work that I do (maybe now it's *did*) there. But, I was worried that maybe some of the people in charge might not get the joke. So, now that chapter has gone down the memory hole.

I'm not used to living in an environment where the worst kept secrets are supposed to remain secret, even though everyone knows that they are true. To me, if it's true and everyone already knows about it, then you should be able to write about it, certainly joke about it, accept it, laugh and move on. Yet, in Croatia there is a lot of face saving at both the personal and institutional level. A lot of times you have to pretend that something isn't the way it really is, even though everyone is aware of the truth.

For example, everyone knows that there exists a subclass of employees called the *honorarci* throughout Croatia. A *honorarac* is a freelance employee that often actually works full-time, but does not have the status of being FULLY EMPLOYED. This is especially the case for people in journalism and media. This employment status matters a lot when it comes to your pension, the amount you pay in taxes, or trying to get a housing loan. And many of Croatia's largest firms employ people as freelancers for years, even though it is not legal to do so for more than three years. I know people who have worked the same jobs in MAJOR firms and institutions for more than a decade as "freelancers." These firms are either rarely ever inspected by the authorities, so the illegality of the workers' status goes unseen, or they use slight changes in the terms of the contract to get out of having to fully employ their *honorarci*.

Being "fully employed" has nothing to do with how much you work, how long you've worked at the job you work, or even how much income you earn. No, none of what should matter matters. What matters is a label that actually only means it's somewhat, sort of, harder to fire you. And this is where accusations of nepotism and corruption come in, because many of those who are "fully employed" are often made so based on the level of their connectivity to the country's power-source-elites. They are the well connected conduits of employment, like copper, and you're rubber.

This employment situation is one of Croatia's biggest problems. I know people who have worked five days a week, eight hours a day at the same job for ten years and are still considered to be officially "freelancers."

And even though we all know, especially those of us in the journalism field, work with or are a *honorarac* we can't and don't write about it, or talk about it, publicly. Instead we talk about it with our friends, listen to the difficulties they have being stuck in a situation that feels both permanent and temporary. And we hope that eventually, someone somewhere will do something about it, even though no one wants to really acknowledge that this problem exists in the first place (sigh).

The level of bullshit that comes out of official offices and institutions in this country is remarkable (not to say that it isn't in the US, but... it's different... er... it was until Trump happened). One of the reasons for this, is again, the country's libel laws. Sometimes when I give an interview the journalist sends me the questions ahead of time. And most of the time after an interview with a newspaper or magazine is done, the journalist sends me the piece for my "authorization." What this means is that I can actually go through the interview and change all the things I said if I don't like them. *What is that?* Now if I change too much, the journalist doesn't have to publish the interview, but if the journalist doesn't send it for authorization, then I, or more likely someone with power and something to lose, can sue them,[3] even if they write that I said the thing that I said. BTW, I have rarely ever changed an interview after a journalist has sent it to me. The only time was when I made a factual error, or when I said something that made absolutely no sense.

In the US no such practice exists, officially. I'm sure there is pressure from the powers-that-be to get journalists to spin things a certain way, or to omit things said on the record, but it is not a daily practice that a politician or celebrity (not that I'm saying I'm a celebrity. I'm less famous and more fame-*ish*) can edit their own interview.

In the 2016 Presidential race, the editorial board for the *Washington Post* released the entire, unedited transcript of an interview they did with Donald Trump. The *New York Daily News* did the same thing with Hillary Clinton. I cannot imagine that happening in Croatia.

---

[3] So, someone might not be able to sue a journalist who doesn't send an interview for authorization, but authorization is in the media law. It's meaning is a bit vague, really? I'm told that many journalists in Croatia send things for authorization just to be sure, and as a "courtesy" inherited from socialism.

At the personal level, face saving goes from a nice form of kindness to a tedious dance where no one can acknowledge the truth. Or, it's a situation where the truth may be inadequate. For example, one day I wanted to let Sara skip school so that we could go get a dog. Vana was absolutely opposed to this idea. I pointed out that it would be on a Tuesday during the second week of her first year of primary school. What could she possibly miss that was so important? Eventually, I felt that Vana's opposition to the idea was more about not wanting to tell the teacher what I just said: *We think getting a dog is more important than attending your class.* I think she believed that to do so could be insulting to her, even though, it is… the truth. I respect everything primary school teachers do, and think they have a very difficult and thankless job (but still not as bad as in America #Iknowmyparentsandsistersareteachers), but I also know that my kid's future was not going to be ruined because she missed the second day of school on her second week (in the end she didn't, but more about the dog later on).

On the other hand, it is nice to consider individuals' feelings before shoving all their faults in their face! One time I gave a talk to the employees at… a um… large furniture store. These employees were from all over the Balkans and so the topic of the talk was how people from different cultures can get along. One of the things I, and some of the audience members, noted was how much more confrontational Americans are than people from this region. Which sounds odd, given that all Americans know about the "Balkans" is war, war, pretty scenery, and war. And yet, we are the assholes! But it's true. It the US we can call people out on their shit with little discretion. We talk back and argue, sometimes politely, sometimes less so. And feelings might be hurt, but if the criticism is apt, then usually, we let it go and move on. Maybe the critic apologizes afterwards. In Croatia, this is one of the biggest mistakes you can make. If you embarrass someone, no matter how accurate or appropriate your criticism is, you will most likely have caused irreparable damage to that relationship. Criticism should come one on one, or... not at all (hopefully there is an exception for expats that write about this stuff in a book).

Now sure, it's probably a good idea not to publicly shame or embarrass people. Using some tact and discretion will probably get better results and create better relationships. But how can you do this with institutions? How can I take an institution aside, like say... a... um... different electric company than the one in Zagreb, and say, "Look, I don't want to hurt your feelings or anything, but you're kind of... over priced and a bit inefficient." You can't!

And this brings us back to why we don't talk or write about all the things everyone knows are true. If we do, we might harm the relationship we have with the very institution, business, politician, political party, or individual whom we hope will one day give us full employment, for a job we are often already doing.

CHAPTER 6

The Hardest Hope

In the fall of my third year living in Croatia, I came home one evening very excited.

"Great news!" I said. "There is another job opening at the College of Political Science!" I was already teaching English to journalism students at the University of Zagreb's Political Science College as an adjunct, and now they had an opening for a full time position. I felt confident I could get the job. I had a BA in English and a PhD in Political Science. On top of my PhD, I was working as a radio journalist for the Voice of Croatia, part of Croatia's national broadcaster, and of course I was writing a semi-popular blog. Not to mention that I was (and still am) a native speaker of the language I'd be teaching, English. And, I was already doing the very job that I would be applying for. For those reasons I was excited, optimistic. *Full time employment at the University!* It would be a dream come true.

"Huh," Vana replied with a heavy air of indifference, barely looking up from her laptop. "You won't get it."

What? Really? Did she not hear the list of things you just read? What the hell?

Now in the US, I would be insulted by such a reply. I would assume that my wife, the love of my life, meant I was unqualified or not good enough to be employed by the University of Zagreb. I would take Vana's comment and feel as if it referred to my own inferiority or incompetence. That's what such a reply would mean to an American in America.

Only, I was an American in Croatia where such a comment doesn't mean that at all. Vana meant no personal offense to me. In fact she was in the act of preparing to elevate me to the position of a martyr. What she was really saying was,

"You *should* get the job, but you won't."

The reason why didn't even need to be stated. In any conversation about work, a job, a promotion, *any* position in Croatia, it is assumed that there are unseen forces conspiring against *you*, the worthy candidate. The network of connections, the web of personal favors that, in so many ways, tethers the society together in small societies like Croatia also works as a cage, a barrier, an obstacle to keep those who are not connected, out, and those who are connected, in. Or at least that's what everyone assumes. The logic goes that the more desirable the position, the tighter the net, and the more necessary the connection.

And this is just some of the shade cast by the cloud of skepticism that hovers over daily life in Croatia. When describing Croatia all kinds of wonderful adjectives fill my head: beautiful, pristine, gorgeous, calm, easygoing, *azure* and yet, lurking among these great images like a shark among a school of radiant fish, is the word skeptical. I'm greeted with skepticism just by living here.

"You live in Croatia?" Some shocked or confused Croatian will ask me, as if she's unsure that she heard right when I said, "I live here." And I'll reply,

"Yes, I live here. In Zagreb." Most often I'm met with a look that either says someone farted or I just placed a losing bet on the wrong horse. Sometimes this look is followed up with a "Why?" Other times we just let the disbelief hang in the air, before awkwardly moving on.

The longer I've lived in Croatia the more I'm confronted with just how much distrust and suspicion shrouds anything beyond your own personal social circle. Friends don't mistrust friends. But, when it comes to those entities that exist just beyond the boundaries of your personal relationships, on the foggy periphery of the unknown, like a swamp mired in the mist of conspiracy, then you never, ever, assume the best. Not only should you assume that the swamp is filled with alligators, you should probably suspect that they've been put there by people who don't like you. Meanwhile, the people they do like, those with *veze* (connections) are secretly given flashlights and a boat. For them, we assume, traversing the swamp is smooth sailing.

So, from Vana's point of view I shouldn't even have bothered applying for the university job, because as a foreigner in Croatia I was about as connectionless as a broken cordless phone. She, and others, were convinced that the position had already been filled by a friend in the minds of the people who matter. But, I couldn't give in. I had to try. Mockingly, I thought *I'm a foreigner in a strange country? Oh no... Ha! We've been here before.* My ancestral DNA started tingling. *Foreigner in a strange country? Why, by golly, that's the heart of the American experience, a story that's the very core of America's optimism and nothing says AMER-I-CA than an overly optimistic belief in ourselves. It's AmeriCAN not AmeriCAN'T!*[4]

The story begins with the pioneers from America's past. If you want to understand the origins of American optimism look at how we look at the immigrant experience.

In 1863 my great-great-great grandfather immigrated to the US from Hannover, Prussia. My great-great uncle, Fritz Sittel was six months old. The family lived in Maryland, on the east coast for about ten years before moving to Indian Territory, which would one day become known as the state of Oklahoma.

Life was tough in the Territory. In a 1933 interview that was part of a deposition in a case for the US Supreme Court, 70 year-old Fritz explained the hardship of his family's life and the rough justice of the Oklahoma frontier.

"Father built a house of boxes and the roof was brush. When it rained mother and I would stand up and become soaked... I remember how my mother used to wish she was back in Maryland, as she was the first white woman to live in McAlester (the "town" they lived in). Few crimes were committed. Punishment was by whipping. For the first offense a man was given thirty-nine lashes; the second, sixty or seventy lashes; and for the third, death—the criminal was tied to a tree and shot. The whipping and shooting were done by the sheriff and his deputies."

---

[4] Unless of course you're talking about restricting access to guns, providing universal healthcare, lowering carbon emissions, limiting corporate campaign contributions and reforming our electoral system. If you're talking about THOSE things, then it seems to be, not just American't, but more like Ameriwon't.

At the same time Fritz recalls how his father, my great--great-great grandfather was able to succeed and prosper.

"Father was a butcher and sold meat to the railroad crew. He would buy his beef and pork from the Indians for very little. Father built rooms to our house, until he made a hotel of it, and called it the 'Elk House.' Father often traveled to buy cattle. He would go on horseback and often carry on his person, as much as $2000,00 in gold and silver."

I have no idea what my great-great-great grandfather's life had been like in Germany, I mean Prussia, but whatever he was, the fact that he brought his family to the US, arrived in America without knowing the language, without knowing many people, having left all of their connections, networks, their very way of life behind in Europe, tells us that he must have believed in the eventuality of his success. Then he went a step further, rather than stay in the congested and overcrowded cities on the East Coast, he went West, into the unknown frontier. To do such a thing you either have to be a fool or an optimist, probably a bit of both.

The American dream is founded on such optimism. It must have taken an enormous amount of hope to get on the boat, cross the ocean and head to a strange land (I know, I did it too. Only, the boat was an airplane and instead of lasting a month the trip lasted 12 hours, but during the flight I think I had to watch *Transformers 2*!). A 19th century trip to the US sounds awful. The ships were cramped and the food was bad. There was no indoor plumbing so everything was done in chamber pots and buckets. Imagine being on a ship crammed with people, tossing and turning on the high seas and everyone doing their business in an unflushable pot, for a month! *Ewww… www… wwww. Ewwww.*

On top of all that, disease was common: cholera, typhus and dysentery killed many of the US's would-be immigrants before they even made it to the American shore. I imagine it took something more than mere hope to endure such conditions on a tiny ship, steaming slowly across the wide expanse of the Atlantic. It must've taken a dream to guide you through the voyage's nightmare and the ever-present fear of the unknown world closing in before you.

Stories similar to my family's are shared all over the United States. Fritz's father immigrated to America, endured the difficulties of Indian Territory and was able to succeed to such an extent that he could carry the equivalent of *45.000 dollars* in today's money on horseback to go buy some cows.

On my father's side, my grandfather came to America in 1911 from Derry, in what would become Northern Ireland. When his father died at an early age, my grandfather became the "man" of the house and went to work. Yet, he was still able to put himself through university and went on to attend Princeton Seminary and become a Presbyterian minister in Pennsylvania.

The contemporary impression of the 19th Century and early 20th Century immigration to the US is largely that it was an experience that began with optimism and concluded with success. It's a nice packaging. And this is the story we Americans have been telling ourselves over and over again. No matter how much the veracity of this American tale has waned in the contemporary United States, this story still defines us and our outlook on life.[5]

When I confront Vana or Croatia's societal skepticism I try to think about the Croatian version of the American story. What did the Croatian experience look like in the 17th, 18th, 19th and 20th centuries. If Americans retell a story of pioneering optimism and eventual, maybe inevitable, success, what do Croatians tell themselves about the past?

As I see it, Croatia has been under various, nondemocratic monarchies in Vienna, Budapest, Venice and Constantinople. There were great territorial fluctuations between each of these entities and the Ottoman Empire. For much of the past Croatia was consistently on the edge of two or more empires, stuck like a Venn diagram in the overlap of their frontiers.

What can one hope to do in such circumstances? Unlike American optimism, hope was not a force used to inspire individual achievement, rather hope served as a shield against misfortune. You likely, *hoped* that nothing horrible would happen more than you hoped you could do something exceptional. As one wiser and older friend explained to me, "It wasn't that there wasn't hope. Croats knew that we would endure, and that things would get better, maybe not in our lifetime, but that it wouldn't be worse, and if they were, we knew we would persevere."

"So, like a kind of negative optimism?" I offer.

"Exactly."

---

[5] Although you can imagine how this narrative neglects the stories of other Americans, like African Americans who came to the US, not as dreamers but as property, as slaves, and American Indians who experienced the arrival of my family more like a nightmare than a "dream."

In the 20th Century you have World War I, the division of an empire by competing nationalizing communities, the dictatorship during the first Yugoslavia, World War II and Fascist rule, then Communism. Say what you will about socialism (and I know there are as many opinions on this topic in Croatia as there are types of rakija), but in most cases achievement was conditioned on one's support of the Party, aka the League of Communists (Quick aside: there is nothing that sounds more menacing to an American than something called the "League of Communists." It reads like something from a comic book, a pantheon of villainy: the Legion of Doom, the Brotherhood of Evil Mutants and… the League of Communists. Cue ominous music: BUM-BUM-BUUUMM. At least the Communist Party had the word party in it, but the League… the League sounds like a group of evil masterminds who meet in a secret, skull-shaped bunker plotting to destroy capitalism… and the world).

One thing about Croatia's position in the world is that often times locals ignored the official rules, since these rules frequently changed along with whichever foreign entity was ruling over that part of the country at that particular time, and were probably quite meaningless to the functions of daily, local life.

Can you imagine going from Ottoman and Italian rulers where there are… you know… *rules,* but not really "rules." And then the Germans (OK Austrians) show up? Then you probably got some goddamn RULES!

But, when you can't have formal rules and institutions, people create informal ones. These are often based on personal relationships, kinship, friendship and things like kumstvo (which is best understood as a system of godfathers and patronage). The role of connections in Croatia and their importance goes back a long way. In the past they necessitated a vital and important role. "Connections" kept society intact amid despotism, turmoil, great upheavals and the imposition of shitty rules from crappy neighbors.

If Americans tell themselves a story in which hope gives our individual initiative enough buoyancy to lift ourselves up in the world, Croatians are told a story where the greatest part of an individual's initiative is sunk by those who exist in an impenetrable world of better connected circumstance. In the US we are encouraged to gaze at the horizon and imagine what lies beyond. In Croatia I hear an old lady telling me that looking so far ahead, well, that'll just strain my eyes.

For good or bad, the United States runs on hope, hope is the oil in the American engine (the fuel is greed and money). In Croatia, it's the opposite. Here, hope drains you. It weakens you, exhausts you, as elements in the system, the mentality, the culture conspire to make you stop, give up and give in. Here, in Croatia, hope is harder.

Nevertheless I was still hopeful. And despite the skepticism of my friends and family, despite everything everyone believes about Croatia, I got the job! And just so you know that I'm not making any of this up, my new job was such an event that it garnered its own article in Croatia's biggest newspaper. The title: "Miracle at the University! A Foreigner Hired!"

This story just sounds like another immigrant story in the American experience: hope at the beginning, success at the end. But, since it's a story of hope and success in

Croatia, well, it has to have a miracle somewhere in the mix. Or, maybe no one else really wanted the job.

CHAPTER 7

Too much chocolate

We are already half an hour late, but we are finally out the door. Sara is finally dressed, Vana has finally found something she feels comfortable wearing, and I've finally convinced both of them that I don't need to wear my heavy coat just because it's cloudy. After all, it is late April. We make it down the apartment's stairs, out the door, and we are almost to the car, I can see it, it isn't far away at all, *we. are. almost. there...* when Vana says:

"Oh damn."

"What?" I ask, thinking I left the iron plugged in, the stove on.

"We didn't get the kids anything!" *Soooo close,* I think. The car now seems like its pulling farther away like the door to sanctuary and safety in some B horror film.

"Well, run to the store," I say. Thank God it's in the bottom of our building. "I'll take Sara and we'll wait in the car." Vana runs to the store. 10 minutes and a steering-wheel-drum-solo later and she emerges with two large chocolate bars and three Kinder eggs.

If you want an algorithm for the kid gift giving code in Croatia, it goes something likes this: chocolate, chocolate, plastic, chocolate, candy, chocolate, plastic. Whenever your kid goes to a friend's house or whenever your kid's friend comes to your house gifts of chocolate and plastic must be given. I imagine it's similar to how life was in the Old West, like in Oklahoma, Indians and Cowboys always brought hides, beads, and maybe hats whenever they met peacefully, but this was done in order to sow reciprocity among two adverse and hostile peoples. In Croatia it's done this way... because. Stop! No, don't try to ask, there are no reasons. Bearing gifts of chocolate and plastic are just another level to the overall culture of gift giving that abounds in Croatia.

In *Chasing a Croatian Girl,* I wrote about how every Croatian house has a little cupboard where all of the given gifts are stowed so that they can be used to be re-gifted at a moment's notice because you never know when you're going to need a gift. The situation is similar with kids. Only, instead of re-gifting a gift we usually go to the store at the last minute and buy some kind of candy or chocolate thing and Kinder eggs, always the *damn* Kinder eggs.

I hate this practice for three reasons, none of which concern the waste of money involved, lest Vana label me "cheap," which BTW is one of the worst things a person can say about you when in the realm of gift giving and hosting. Friendship is not the place to flex fiscal responsibility in Croatia. You want to do that? You do that with your own stuff, never for friends! And that's actually kind of nice, until of course you buy half a kilo of cheese, equal parts pršut, four bags of chips, three loaves of bread and 20 beers, only to have Vana shake her head and glare, and say: "Are you sure it's enough?" And this is for three guests who may or may not come over and stay long enough to eat something. Answer: In Croatia it's never enough.

OK, back to the list of why I don't like giving kids things (And why I hate sunshine, snowflakes and Christmas! I don't hate any of those things, really): *Reason number 1:* Food in Croatia is very healthy. The vegetables are fresh, nothing has high fructose corn syrup in it, which is in everything in the US, even the bread! Very little of what we cook and eat is processed... And yet, we give our kids tons and tons of chocolate. It's paradoxically frustrating!

Reason number 2: It makes us too indulgent towards our kids. Not only am I being amicable enough to let Sara's friends come scream, play, and trash our apartment for 2-3 hours, I'm letting this happen with kids I can barely speak to in Croatian. That this is allowed should be a big enough "gift" on its own. All I really need is to have these kids wired on tons of chocolate, which I can't stop them from eating because I don't know how to say, "Hey stop eating all that chocolate," in Croatian.

Reason number 3: Kinder eggs are awful. They're even banned in the US. For a long time this has been a puzzle. I mean why would you ban a chocolate egg filled with a plastic toy and not ban something like an AR15 assault rifle? Answer, because a chocolate egg filled with a plastic toy is the worst thing ever!

The toy is useless and entertains your kid for about, oh say, five seconds. Usually you have to assemble it via instructions that are depicted with less-than-clear microscopic drawings. So, after ten minutes of painstaking effort, for which even the thinnest adult fingers are too large to snap *this* plastic tab into *that* one or to place this pinky-nail-sized decal on a car the size of your index finger, you finally give it to your kid, who you know is used to stuff like video games, and she's a bit disappointed. And how can she not be... it's a plastic toy, assembled out of a chocolate egg! *Ooo. Wow. Ah.*

Now you're stuck with random, broken, bits of plastic egg toys that don't seem to conform to one organizational category. So, you end up with a shoebox of Kinder egg toy composites. Though those little things are impossible to put together, they easily fall apart. They never stay complete, leaving you with just the bits and pieces of what was once an already disappointing toy. And after years of this (remember every time any friend comes over) you begin finding bits of Kinder egg toys all over the place, under the couch, in a shoe, in your desk drawer, for some reason in your coat pockets. At the store I reach into my coat for change and come up with the flotsam and jetsam of a Kinder toy. It's as if they secretly multiply after midnight like some kind of German made *Mogwai*.

What's more, turns out they cause cancer! I'm not lying about this. In July 2016 a chemical that the European Food and Safety authority labels as carcinogenic was found to be above the acceptable safety levels in Kinder chocolate. So, there you go: Screw these ridiculous, messy, plastic strewing cancer eggs!

If you live in America, thank the nameless bureaucrat that banned Kinder eggs. It's the greatest piece of policy to come out of Washington in years.

4) *Reason number 4:* As someone who believes good parenting involves making decisions my daughter's five-

year-old impulsive brain isn't capable of making, I, of course, try to limit her intake of sweets and chocolate. What this means is that every time a friend or one of our friends comes over and gives her chocolate, in reality they are giving *me* chocolate. We stash the chocolate in a cabinet in the living room, and there it sits like a temptress, calling to me between meals, after a meal, with every cup of coffee.

Come on Cody, it's just one bit of chocolate...

Shut up cupboard chocolate!

Oh come now, I thought we were friends...

No! We're not friends and you're— you're the devil!

Mmmm I bet the crappy ole instant coffee would taste better with a piece of nice, dark, smooth cho-co-late...

Back SATAN! The power of Christ compels... oh fuck it!

I give in. A nibble here. A nibble there. Next thing I know I'm surrounded by a pile of wrappers with an opaque stream of nougat dangling off of my chin.

It's like gifting Sara of a pack of cigarettes. Of course I won't let her smoke them, but then, since I'm a former, still sometimes, smoker, I end up smoking them. I've tried different ways to combat the chocolate problem. One day I decided the only way to get rid of it all was just to eat all of it in one day. Didn't work. Next day, a friend from out of town visited, she brought more chocolate. There is actually a correlation between the distance one travels and the amount of chocolate they bring. Someone from Split is likely to bring a whole gigantic chocolate bar, Kinder egg, and a pack of cookies.

After a frenzy of binging on delicious cupboard chocolate I can still look in the mirror without an inkling of shame. *This*, I think as I look myself up and down in the large mirror in our hallway, as I study my ever expanding middle-age-waistline, *this, is called taking one for the team*. By eating the chocolate I'm ensuring that Sara won't eat it. I've managed to convince myself that my indulgence isn't a vice. It's the opposite. It's good parenting!

I know, I know this probably doesn't sound like a real problem. *Oh my God, Cody, you poor thing, Croatia sounds horrible, people keep bringing you chocolate. How awful.* Yeah, well you'll change your tune when you start splitting the seats of your pants!

The quantity of junk food we allow our kids to eat is not just a result of friends coming over. When it comes to kids, there is always an urgency to eating. Croatian parents are constantly preoccupied with the hunger status of their kid. And there is no gray area here, your kid is never "kind of" hungry, or a little bit hungry. Sort of hungry? No, a child is either hungry or not. It's binary code, 0 or 1. And if it's the former, then that child needs food STAT!

After school, especially in the spring, summer and fall, my daughter and her classmates always play in the little park beside their preschool. It's a great time. The kids hang, the parents talk, there is even a cafe close enough that we can have coffee or beer and keep an eye on the kids. But we are confronted with the parents' dilemma. Do we feed the kids something unhealthy from the store or bakery, or do we let them starve to death on the playground. Fine. It's not really a dilemma. Inevitably we buy them ice cream, or hotdogs, or chocolate croissants, all of which feed into the indulgent, unhealthy habits we are instilling in our kids.

At one point Mirko, father of Sara's best friend, remember, has had enough. He's sick of feeding our kids impulsive junk food. He's going to take matters into his own hands! And he does. One day he makes homemade grilled chicken sandwiches. And that's Croatia, where a parent makes sandwiches for *all* the kids. They look good. They smell good. They have all the rudiments of a nice sandwich: chicken, some cheese, a bit of mayo and a couple slices of tomato.

After school that day Sara and, his daughter Nora, whine about how hungry they are. They drag their feet, too exhausted to go one step further.

"You're hungry?" Mirko asks, sardonically.

"Starving!" They moan collectively.

"Great! I've made sandwiches for everyone!" A shadow of confusion falls across their faces. *Sandwiches? Huh?* You can see the question on their brows, *What about chocolate croissants? Kinder eggs? Ice cream?* Mirko unpacks the sandwiches. Each one is wrapped in aluminum foil. The "starving" children look on in odd fascination. Sara takes a tentative bite. She's like Wicket the Ewok cautiously accepting a cracker from Princess Lea in *Return of the Jedi*.

Mirko is beginning to bask in the glow of Dad triumph. He smiles. He's done it. I'm impressed too. But then, a few more hesitant bites into the sandwich, and...

"Daddy," Sara says. "I don't like this. I want a chocolate croissant."

"I want ice cream."

"A Kinder egg!"

"A hotdog!" And the playground descends into a cacophony of whining, beseeching children. Mirko and I stand strong. We make a joint declaration like two proconsuls in Rome giving dictates to a crowd of Plebeians.

"Sandwiches or nothing!" The kids quiet down, considering, they look at each other. And they choose... nothing. Sara hands me her sandwich.

"Here." She says, running off to play. Mirko is crestfallen. His plan is but the ruins of bread crumbs, strings of crumpled foil and three partially eaten sandwiches. I take a bite, happy to have a good sandwich.

"This is a good sandwich," I say, but it sounds like "Misses a mood sambich," with my mouth full and I don't think my mumbled compliments cheer Mirko up. In the air of sullen disappointment, we watch the kids play. They swing, they spin on that thing that spins, they conspire like future grownups.

Then the kids return, like a little gang of lawyers and diplomats. They've conferred with each other. And they're ready to negotiate. We make a deal, half a sandwich and then some ice cream, but the smallest ice cream.

Well, I think, *it was a worthy effort.* I'm still holding the other half of Sara's sandwich. I take another bite and chew. And I'm happy that at least this time, it's not chocolate.

CHAPTER 8

Buying an apartment is... difficult

We are on time, but the real-estate agent is late. I get out of the car to observe our surroundings. Though we are in Zagreb it hardly feels like it. A lonely apartment block is all that stands nearby. The area has the feeling of a failed suburban development, something that in America would've been a plan of homes and succulent ovals on the expanding edge of town, with rows of housing lots, and just a smattering of homes on cul-de-sac streets. Only where its abandonment would have come from the housing crash in the US, this place's bareness lingers from the collapse of Yugoslavia. It's not so much undeveloped as it is stuck in a time that was supposed to have stopped existing. Only, it didn't. People still live here. Time moves on and the grass grows and dries between the cracks of the craggy parking lot.

There is a very odd air about the place. In a city known for its cafes there isn't a single one in sight. There is no kiosk, no grocery store, nor a hair salon. All of which I've come to think as the ubiquitous pieces of Zagreb's geography. Cafes, kiosks, hair salons, and bakeries are to

Zagreb what the sand is to the desert. You just can't have one without the other. We arranged with the realtor to look at some apartments in a certain area of town in a certain price range. Instead she insisted on meeting us here, in an area we've never heard of. And so, here we are in some incomplete no-man's land, on a winter morning, waiting for the realtor to show us an apartment I'm pretty sure we aren't interested in buying.

Since I've become fully employed, we've decided it's time to buy an apartment. I'm optimistic because that's my job as an American in Croatia. Everyone else is jumping to share their horror stories about apartment buying. They make it sound dreadful, awful, humiliating and frustrating. Turns out... they're right.

Property (meaning land, homes, apartments, buildings, spaces) is like a microcosm of Croatian dysfunction. It's the petri dish on which all specimen of Croatia's problems grow. Property combines the unresolved complications of Croatia's past with the dual nature of the state's legal system, which itself moves from oddly ambiguous to fiercely rigid. Property encompasses the economic malaise burdening the society. Property highlights the failure of the country's political class and policymakers to actually improve Croatia, while at the same time demonstrating exactly why nothing can be made better without first making everything worse. Property is the nightmare from which Croatia is trying to awake.

And I blame the Commies! There, I said it. Private property is the source of all evil in the Communist ideology. It's like communism's Cthulhu. And yet, when you think about it, private property is why we have any equality under the law *at all*. Find a repressive state and you'll find weak property laws. North Korea, Myanmar, Russia, um... lots of Africa. Ironic isn't it? The movement that most preached about equality actually undermined its very principles by getting rid of private property.

The great political theorist John Locke wrote that humans had three inviolable rights: life, liberty and property. The American Founding Father Thomas Jefferson later paraphrased this to "Life, Liberty and the pursuit of happiness." The reason for Locke's emphasis on property came from events happening in England. See, once some folks in England had accumulated enough stuff to attract the attention of their "betters," namely the King and the Church, the royals or clergy came along like some school yard bullies and said: "Hey, nice stuff. Mind if I see it?"

It was the classic schoolyard trick, where by see, the bullies mean see with their hands and not with their eyes. Next thing you know and... "Now it's mine!"

And that's why England (and America) developed property laws to tell the Kings and the priests that they just can't take rich people's stuff. And from this idea, plus a lot of hard work on behalf of high minded individuals and the organized masses, restrictions were placed on the King, i.e., the state, which brings us to the modern social contract and democracy. But since people also had to give up *some* of their property in the form of taxes, they said to the King/state,

"Well, we'll give you some taxes, but you have to let us in on the decision making. We want a government and we want to be able to say how you can spend our money" (actually, few people in Croatia say this. Usually they just shrug and sort of say *meh* with their eyes). And just like that, KA-CHING! the whole rationale for governmental accountability and public involvement in the governing process was born! TADA! Democracy! And all because people wanted to keep (most of) their stuff.

But it wasn't so for the Communists. Since private property was Marx's be-all and end-all of evil... (ironically, it wasn't the overly centralized, authoritarian state, ruled by a dictator in a single party), socialist states, like Yugoslavia, did not have the strongest laws on property. Walk around, talk to some Croatians and you'll find someone who is still dealing with this issue today. Namely they are trying to get something back that the Communists took from their family, or they are trying to keep something that the Communists lent or sold to someone in their family (and its usually something they live in). Or they are just trying to figure who owns what. I'm convinced that the lack of strong laws on private property, the simple who owns what, how and why, contributes to the overall weakness and inefficiency of Croatia's institutions. It also makes looking for an apartment an incredible pain in the ass (#firstworldproblemsbutstillpostsocialistproblems).

The agent finally shows up and insists on showing us one of the apartments in the lonely housing block. We try to explain that we aren't really interested. I mean if I wanted to live in the middle of nowhere in a city, I'd just move back to Oklahoma. Nevertheless the owner pulls up 10 minutes later to show us the apartment with the agent. Vana and I both feel awkward that this guy had to return from *wherever* just to show us an apartment we know we aren't going to buy. He is nice and hopeful, which makes it even worse.

Exploring someone else's home for just a few minutes is a bit thrilling. It's like spying briefly on how someone else lives. I wonder if this is what thieves feel when they break into someone's home. We walk through the apartment, trying to look at the space and not the relics of the owner's life, but you can't really prevent yourself from trying to tell a story from the furniture, toys, and other bits of the mundane that our existence consists of.

The agent is right, the apartment is nice, but it is also overpriced and not at all what we want. But I feel for her and for the family trying to sell it. The agent has to try, and I guess she's hoping that upon seeing its "OK-ness" we will suddenly abandon all of our own criteria and announce: *We'll take it*. Alas, we won't.

None of the other apartments we see that day, though more to our liking, really do it for us. And the odd sensation of entering someone's home continues during our whole apartment hunting odyssey. It's coupled with some just baffling behavior on the part of the owners. Though their apartments are for sale, it seems like they aren't trying to *sell* anything.

Many of the apartments we visit are in horrible shape. The life of an apartment in Croatia can resemble the life cycle of a piece of fruit. When the apartment is new, up until just after it's ripe, the original owners live in it. Then, once the apartment begins to turn like a piece of rotting fruit, they rent it. As it grows more and more rotten, they begin to rent it to students. A "student apartment" implies that it's in bad shape, poorly or barely maintained in some sort of agreement where the students can do what they want as long as they don't require the landlord to fix it. And then, once the fruit/apartment is too rotten even for students, the owners decide to sell it. But they don't charge the rotten fruit price, because as they see it, you're not buying just the fruit, you're buying a part of the tree. And this means that you'll have to pay too much for an apartment that you're supposed to gut, and rebuild from the inside out. It's a case of expectations and reality passing each other like two ships on a foggy night.

And those owners who do bother to fix up their place are even more discouraging. Some beam with pride at some horrible "improvement." Like placing the cheapest strips of laminate haphazardly over the original wood floor. At these moments you can't tell if the owner is trying to dupe you into thinking these slipshod repairs are really quality, or maybe the owner himself has been duped by someone else. In most cases we leave each apartment in a state of pity, anxiety, and bewilderment.

It seems as if no one really wants to move, or if they do they aren't in a hurry about it. One lady wants us to buy her apartment, pay her the full amount, and wait a few years until her dog dies, then she'll move. Other people seem mostly interested in asking for a price just to see what happens.

The saddest situations are those involving the elderly. The generation born before or during World War II, but raised under socialism has been squeezed the hardest in Croatia's turbulent transitions. Promised that the state would take care of them, they worked only to hit retirement just as privatization upended everything, the only thing these people have in their possession is their apartment. Only, some of these places have deteriorated to a state of near decay: flaking paint, creeping mold, and oddly, a really, really large number of plants in the kitchen. Of course the apartment's state is not born out of the owners' negligence, but because in their old age they are unable to maintain it themselves, and in their post-socialist poverty they are unable to afford to pay for the necessary repairs. And since it's all that they have, they have to ask for full price, and since all we have is just enough to buy the place, we can't possibly offer them full price. Each time we leave one of these apartments I can see that the owners are stuck, rooted by circumstance to the past in an increasingly uncertain present.

Then, after months of looking, we found our dream apartment!... Or... (head turns sideways, eyebrows up, voice rising)... did we?

The apartment was a spacious place on the top floor (with an elevator!) of a socialist housing block near where we were already living. While so many of the other places we'd seen had had the feeling of a horribly aged piece of cheese, green and black around the edges, this place was open, well lit and marvelously pleasant. Built in the 1950s, it was designed in the style of midcentury modern. Socialist brutalism hadn't yet come into vogue. It had lots of windows with a nice view of Trešnjevka and a relatively open floor plan. Since it was on the top floor it even had angled ceilings that gave the apartment an air of elegance from a forgotten time, like a black and white photograph. It seemed like the kind of place you could entertain the Rat Pack, had they made a trip to 1960s Yugoslavia.

I wanted to put on a bossanova record and drink a Manhattan while wearing a sharkskin suit. None of which I had ever done or dreamed of doing before, but this apartment had an infective and inspiring kind of style about it. It was even designed by one of Croatia's most famous architects. I felt like it was a writer's place, an artist's space, it was just the kind of place in which you wanted to live.

The fact that it was in a historically socialist apartment block appealed to my inner dissident, even though I was also cursing the effects of communism on property, I still liked to rebel against the system: *Take that America! I'm living in a building built for Communists! And in style!*

What more could I want? Everything was going to be all right.

And then the crushing reality of the ineptitude and ambiguity of the Croatian legal and political system fell on our dreams like an anvil on an egg: crunch, squish, splat! That's the sound your housing dreams make in Croatia: Crunch! Squish! *SPLAT!*

The problem was that the owner had made some, um, renovations that weren't exactly "legal." He'd extended his entranceway into the stairwell, which sounds shitty towards the other residents in the apartment building, but since his apartment was the only apartment on the top floor, its expansion didn't really come at the expense of the other tenants in the building. Next, he'd inclosed some balconies that aren't called balconies in Croatian, even though Croatian has the word "balkon" which means balcony. The balconies in this apartment (and in many other apartments) were some kind of hybrid balcony-room-space referred to as a "lođa." The apartment's owner had extended the kitchen out onto one of the "lođa."

Now, you might be thinking, so what? People make renovations to their places all the time. Yes, but in Croatia a lot of people make renovations without the proper paper work and permits. Why? Well, because getting everything in order is a very complicated affair. In some cases all of the tenants of the apartment building have to agree. In other cases, there is a big delay because, well, bureaucracy. In the worst cases either another tenant or a bureaucrat is holding out for a bribe. Ergo, some people just take the initiative and try to retroactively legalize their renovations.

A lot of the trouble goes back to the fact that during socialism all of the property was technically owned by the state. State firms built their own apartment buildings and then distributed the apartments to their workers. In the 1990s the apartments were privatized and most people were able to buy the apartment they were living in from the state. However, there is still a little hiccup in that as far as I understand it, you actually don't own an apartment in what was once state property, rather you own a percentage of the building (I think, it's very confusing, obviously). This fact seems to get in the way of doing renovations in your apartment without the approval of all the other tenants, because in some cases you could be expanding the percentage of your ownership.

And it's about to get even more complicated. The owner of the apartment-we-loved had "legalized" all of his renovations, which you would think solved the problem. Nope, turns out the term "legalized" is just a term that means different things to different people. Like justice, equality or middle class, the term legalized is so ambiguous and grand that you could imagine toga wearing philosophers debating its meaning. *Yes, but what does it mean to be... legalized? Hmm (white beard stroking, strikes a thoughtful pose).*

The owner said that it meant the expansions and additions could never be taken away, or reverted to what they had been. Others, like a friend who was a lawyer, said she wasn't so sure that that was exactly what that meant. At some point in the future, she warned, we might have to pay for the expansion. How much? No idea. When? No idea. And the likelihood? No idea. The craziest thing of all is that the renovations had expanded the apartment from 72 square meters to 87 or maybe even 98 square meters (more on this discrepancy in a minute), but if we bought the apartment we would only be able to "own" the original 72 square meters, even though we would be living in the additional space. *What does that even mean!?! How is that even possible!?!*

APARTMENT BUYING IN CROATIA: DEFYING THE LAWS OF PHYSICS SINCE 1991!

As for the 87 or 98 square meters. The architecture firm that "legalized" the apartment, remember we don't really know what that means, decided to add the gross square meterage, meaning all the area in the apartment if, for some inexplicable reason, someone decided to knock down ALL the walls, which no one had done. So, we couldn't even be sure to what extent the expansions had actually expanded the apartment. And in Croatia this is incredibly important since taxes and sometimes your heating bill are determined according to the number of your apartment's square meters.

In the end it would be technically possible for us to buy and own 72 square meters of the apartment, while really living in its 87 square meters, and paying taxes on a 98 square meter apartment, but still receiving heating bills for only the original 72 square meter apartment. Crunch, squish, splat.

Apartment buying on our budget in Croatia was like a Quixotic quest. It had the trappings of tragedy, but often felt like farce. Each time one piece of the complicated and ambiguous puzzle was resolved, each time we got some document, a stamp, an official response from a state institution or the owner, each time the mists of Croatia's bureaucratic fog thinned and parted just enough for us to glimpse the horizon and our goal, another thick layer of mist would come rising out of nowhere. Something else would come along and cast us back into a world of ignorance and uncertainty. It was like peeling an onion grown in Kafka's garden, searching for a reliable core that just wasn't there.

CHAPTER 9

A Real Friend Is a Skeptic

In September 2013 I signed the book contract for *Chasing a Croatian Girl*. Now, telling someone you are writing your first book is a lot like telling someone you're composing an opera. They assume you're not really that serious, and if you are, then at least you won't ever finish it, and if you do, few people will listen to it. The difference between America and Croatia is that in America everyone assumes these things, silently. In Croatia everyone tells you these things, repeatedly.

I meet a friend, the editor of the culture section for a newspaper, in a cafe on Savska.

"So, how are you?" She asks, her eyes sparkle with what's either real interest or real mischief.

"Great," I say. "The book's almost done. I think it will be great when it comes out." She gives me a long, lasting glance and says,

"You know, bestselling books sell like 500 copies in Croatia. Even major authors only sells a few hundred copies."

"I think we'll sell more," I reply politely.

"..." My friend inhales her cigarette, exhales. And then some damage control.

"Look, I'm sure the book will be great, but people here just don't read or buy books."

What? Oh wait, is that you, skepticism. I didn't recognize you. Yes, no matter what you do, say, or believe, Croatians are ready to wrap themselves in the protective armor of skepticism. *Can't be disappointed if every glass is always gonna be half empty!*

And they try to wrap you in that armor too. They just want to grip your soul and shove it into a cast of encasing steel and iron, anything to protect a naive American from the disappointing reality that is life!

Once we find an apartment that we want to buy and it looks like it might actually work this time, Mirko advises me on all the reasons why we shouldn't.

"That's a lot of money," he says.

"I know, but it's the same price as your apartment."

"Yeah, but our apartment..."

"Is in the same building as the one we want to buy and was in worse condition."

"I know, but I'm just saying," hands up palms out as if he's placing this statement in the middle of the table.

"You never know what can happen in this country," he says. His hands withdraw, as if to say, *there, I said it*.

Yes, a Croatian friend is like an infinite reservoir of expertise. They are an expert on why whatever it is you want to do will likely fail. But, don't take this the wrong way. Again, it's not because your friend doesn't believe in you. It's because your friend doesn't believe in the fairness, justice, or any good fortune in the system, world, or universe, especially if it involves anything in Croatia out of your immediate circle of friends. Advising someone to take caution, explaining why they shouldn't follow their dreams is Croatia's highest form of friendship. It's the real, honest expression of concern and the feeling that your friend is in some way responsible for your success and failures (or at least that's the only reason I can explain why my wife's friends advised her NOT to marry me).

In America, it's different. We don't care what stupid scheme our friend comes up with, or who they marry, because we are not going to consider ourselves responsible for his idiotic screw-up. Do you think any of John DeLorean's friends tried to warn him about making the DeLorean? For those that don't remember or forgot, the DeLorean DMC-12 was a unique car manufactured in the early 1980s. Its stainless steel body and gull-wing doors made the car look like it was from the future. In fact the DMC-12 was the car from the film *Back to the Future*. In any case, DeLorean's friends probably didn't warn him about how stupid his car idea was. He was all like, "and the doors are gonna open like this." Whatever, that's great John. Do you think Steve Job's friends advised him against making the Apple Newton? No. And again, if you don't remember the Newton, it was like your smart phone, but without apps, the Internet, or phone service. Though, you could write notes on it with a specialized stylus!

In America you take chances at your own peril. You are on your own. In Croatia, however, once we are friends we become bounded with complicated burdens, each of us is our brother's keeper. Indifference is not a luxury friends can afford. So, when you announce your ridiculous idea, like writing a book, buying an apartment, changing careers, any idea in which the probability of success is scant... well, your friend is gonna be right there to tell you that the odds are not, and likely never will be, in your favor.

My friends were just trying to protect me from disappointment, and, or ruin. I think that since I was an American they felt that they *really* had to warn me about how horrible Croatia was. A horror I found lacking in fright and terror, but quite plentiful in frustrations. Croatia had yet to be scary, scary like say getting a terminal illness without insurance or having-a--family-to-support-without-health-insurance-in-America scary, or dark-alley-in-New Orleans-ghetto-scary. No, Croatia was definitely not skinny, white, bugged-eyed, nervous meth-dealer on Route 66 kind of scary. When it came to my book I was more scared of not finishing something I was proud of than I was about not selling very many copies.

Once the book came out I liked to go by as many bookstores as I could and look at it. I would often bring Sara.

At the mall I'm guiding her by the hand and she's asking me,

"Daddy where are we going?"

"Upstairs real quick."

She groans, and begins to drag her feet. "I don't want to go look at your book!"

"Just for a minute."

"Why do we have to look at your book every time we go somewhere?" Sure, part of me is ashamed that I'm so obsessed with my success that I have to go look at my book all the time. The other part is also proud that I have the privilege to drag a four-year-old through the shopping mall, her legs refusing to bend, noises of resistance sounding from her as if I'm taking her to the doctor for a vaccination, all so we can go look at my book in the front window of the bookstore.

And there it stands, one displayed on a little book easel, with rows upon rows of *my book*, stacked behind the glistening glass of the display case, perched right up front for the whole world to see. I swear if I listen intently, blocking out Sara's protests, I can hear a choir of angels, singing "ahhhhhhhhh." It looks majestic as the luminous beams of the mall's fluorescent light shine down upon the scene.

Success! Right? The book was a bestseller! I didn't need my friends' armor or cautionary advice after all. And here is where the story ends and it all wraps up nicely? Struggling immigrant arrives in country, writes a successful bestselling book about his new homeland. *Damn. It's like America itself wrote this story.* So this is the part where I raise my arm in triumph and the credits begin to roll while playing *Don't You* by Simple Minds... Wait. Wait. Wait. Stop the music, wrap the credits back. This scene can happen in another story about another country, or in one about suburban high schoolers in Saturday detention in the 1980s, ... but that story cannot happen here.

A few months after the book was published, my publisher entered into pre-bankruptcy procedure. It's what the British call a Voluntary Company Agreement, and in the US is referred to as Chapter 11, but in Croatia they use the frightening phrase *pre-bankruptcy procedure*! Leave it to the Croatians to pick the most pessimistic or "negatively optimistic" name. No matter what country we are talking about, it meant my publisher need to restructure their debt. Yeah. That's right.

And right now, I imagine there is some kind of grim satisfaction among my Croatian readers. A smile forming at the corners of your mouth? A little voice saying *Aha!* Well, you, my friend, are not alone. Once I heard the news about my publisher's financial insolvency I told Mirko, and he responded in an entirely appropriate way.

He laughed.

We were in the park. Our daughters were swinging and we were just standing around like bored parents do.

"My publisher just entered pre-bankruptcy procedure," I said. And instead of saying something like:

"Oh man, that sucks." A knowing smile just spread across Mirko's face.

"See?" He said. "See? You see how it goes here." Behind the smile was a knowing look, a kind of respect actually, a sparkle in the eyes that all seemed to say "now you're one of us." *You've been screwed by circumstance! Welcome to Croatia!* I imagine that somewhere there could be a store selling t-shirts with this slogan: *I know I'm Croatian because I've been screwed by circumstance.*

What could I do? This was a problem, it sucked, but it wasn't a crisis for me. My publisher was financially insolvent and I couldn't really blame them. Croatia's economy is one of the worst in Europe and the book industry is dying globally (put down your smartphones people!). It just seemed like I had published a book a lot of people happen to like at the wrong time. As a friend once said in the face of much, much bigger problems: *life sucks, get a helmet*. I was more worried about all the people that worked for my publisher and the bookstore. My book was just a side source of income. These people had jobs! These people had helped publish my book in the first place. What about them?

Of course a lot of other people refused to see it this way. While financial difficulties seemed normal for a publisher and bookstore chain in a country with such an anaemic economy as Croatia's (*Books! Last century's great idea!*), other people chose to see yet another conspiracy, another instance of better connected people trying to take advantage of everyone else. And that got quite tiresome. Of course behind these assumptions there was no element of outrage, no violence, no shame even. Rather, there was just this placid, resignation that said, *Yep, but this is just how it goes. This is Croatia.*

But is it? Or is the default setting just to assume the worst? At the university I often see how my students are conflicted. Many of them want to work hard, study and learn how to be a journalist or a political scientist, and yet at the same time they don't really see what the point is. Many of them believe that their employment will rely less on their skills and experience and more on the connections they have with whomever is hiring. Now, there might be some truth to this, but the common refrain that you need a connection to get a job seems exaggerated.

How exactly does having a "connection" and employment work? Is it truly someone calling someone else while smoking a cigar and saying in an old time gangster accent: "Hey, look here see, I need you to hire my cousin. Do it and you won't be sorry." Or is a connection more like a personal reference. Someone in the know, knows someone, who knows someone who knows you and says, "Hey, here's a gal that I can recommend." If it's a reference, than that suggests Croatia is just a real life version of the social network LinkedIn, except Croatia actually does what LinkedIn pretends to do. I believe it's likely to be a bit of both.

Whenever my students are subsumed with despair about their future careers and lack of connectivity, I ask them if their parents aren't hard workers? Do their parents only have jobs through some connection? Or are they decent, qualified people? Of course the answer is usually that their parents are hard workers who are not employed simply through some connection. My students seem to believe that there is at least some merit-based reason for their own parents' employment.

The really weird thing is that amid all of this skepticism and pessimism Croatia has social values I wish America could embody. After living here five years, I'm convinced Americans and Croatians are socially different. We act and behave differently. Americans may value individualism and entrepreneurship, but by doing so I feel we devalue community and empathy. Sure there is a lot of talk about cherishing "community," but there is a huge gap between our talk and our reality. This has become increasingly clear after living in Croatia.

Croatia is one of the poorest countries in the EU, and yet the society here has decided that education and healthcare should be freely available to everyone. *Free...* er at least moderately affordable. Sure, lots of other countries offer similar social goods, but these countries are also high on the list of developed economies, Croatia isn't. To me it speaks volumes about the type of society we have here, even amid scarce resources healthcare and education are free, or at least low-cost. The me-first-attitude doesn't seem to be as prevalent among the public as it is in the US. *Me first:* The motto of America. You can imagine what it must've been like getting off that boat. *First off the boat wins!*

The social values in Croatia may seem dormant because Croatians don't seem to enjoy bragging about themselves that much, unless you are talking about food and athletics. Then, Croatians are all full of pride. Just say *štrukle* and people beam with a proud happiness. Even if healthcare and education policy are just examples of the empathetic nature of Croatia, empathy pulses through our relationships in this country. Friendship and family are actually two things that Croatians hold very dear. You, honestly, cannot say "no" to family. Even when your cousin announces he is coming to stay for the weekend in your two bedroom apartment while your mother-in-law and a friend from the US are also visiting! All you can do is smile and say: *Greeeeeaaaaat!*

Meanwhile, in the massive American economy, healthcare and education are the two biggest reasons individuals go into massive debt. Medical debt is the number one cause of bankruptcy in the US. And you can say no to friends and family requests. So, even though I can complain about the corruption in Croatia, one way to look at corruption here, is that it's just a friend or family member refusing to refuse a request.

Of course I don't like the corruption (Who does? Oh wait, politicians. I forgot), but I also want my daughter to live in an empathetic society. One where she can grow up with concern for her neighbors or her neighbors' concern for her (and trust me there is a lot of neighborly concern in Croatia, from friends who are neighbors to that old lady that watches the street through a set of partially parted curtains). I want her to live in a place where she can understand that success is not just dependent on individual initiative, rather it is influenced on circumstance and contingencies. And while this may seem obvious to people all over the world, to Americans it isn't. *For real*. Look at these numbers:

A 2011 Pew Research Poll showed that 58 percent of Americans believe it is more important for individuals to have "the freedom to pursue life's goals" than it is to support government policies that "leave no one in need" (36 percent were for the latter). A comparison to other, European countries' responses is revealing: Britain supported the statement about freedom with 38 percent, Germany, 36; France, 36; Spain, 30. Whereas responses to "leaving no one in need" were in Britain, 55; Germany, 62; France, 64; and Spain, 67. In a related poll, only 36 percent of Americans believe "Success in life is determined by forces outside our control."

In the US we have the social myth that poverty is somehow a choice, and it's a choice for which you should be punished. If you're poor, you deserve to go to a bad school and have limited healthcare, maybe then you'll chose to become rich like all the good, worthy people. And this is one explanation for how Donald Trump became president.

Of course this attitude can go back to our good old pioneering story that we tell ourselves again and again. The necessity for optimism in America's early years has reinforced the belief among us Americans that we are an "exceptional" people. Yet, this exception does not come from the "nation" in the European sense. It is not an exclusive club defined by bloodlines and ethnic identity.

Rather, it is just the opposite. It is exceptional because it is a dream that Americans believe is transferable to all those who want to believe.

The exceptionality of the "American Dream" is more a form of religious conversion than a nationalist or patriotic position. Exceptionalism may be constrained to the US's geography and culture, but it is not constrained to a specific nation or culture (white supremacists and racists would argue otherwise of course, but for the most part I think Americans believe in the universality of their own uniqueness). Poverty in America is seen as a form of individual failure. And this failure is rarely seen as a product of circumstance, rather it is viewed as the embodiment of one's wavering faith in the American Dream. In the US, the poor present a challenge. The existence of the impoverished is either evidence that the American Dream is not a reality, but rather a myth, or, American poverty is the evidence of an individual's own failure. Since our whole identity is predicated on the promise of America we collectively prefer the later. Thus the poor, the weak and the down trodden are hated and shunned like heretics.

Socially, we are at an impasse. Croatians are some of the most skeptical people when it comes to the state and condition of their country. And yet, it's still a very nice place, and in my opinion, possesses something the US lacks, social empathy and strong social ties. Sure, with the political class there are a lot of examples of corruption, but there are just as many examples in other countries (ahem * cough * lobbyists). A lot of what goes on in Croatia as "corruption" is just "politics" in America. I mean what else can you call billionaires giving millions to political campaigns?

The public's belief in how each society functions in Croatia and the US are at opposite ends of the spectrum. In the US personal advancement is seen as something completely detached from circumstance, and in Croatia personal advancement is seen mostly as a condition of circumstance, *vis a vis* connections. Croatians are overly pessimistic and Americans may be overly optimistic.

Sometimes, I feel like climbing up to Zagreb's upper town and yelling from the hillside: "Croatians! The glass might be half full!" And then back in the US, I want to shout from the Empire State building: "America! A lot of people can't even afford the god-damn glass!" Like a zen master in some cartoon about martial arts might say, I suppose it's all about balance.

And since you're now reading a new book published by the same people, you can see that in the end it all worked out.

Take that skeptics!

CHAPTER 10

Missing America

One day in the late Spring, Sara and I go to Bundek Lake in Zagreb. On the way to the park from the parking lot, I see what looks like people playing baseball. I don't believe it. Baseball? Here in Croatia? I stand there transfixed. Sara is pulling on my hand, trying to get me to move, saying "come on, come on," pedestrians are giving me weird looks as they have to walk around us. I don't care, nothing matters, I just want to watch the game.

Now, the weird thing is that I don't even really like baseball. In fact, the sport and I have an unpleasant history. At some point in his life, every Midwestern, American boy has to play baseball, regardless of talent or skill. For the kids who were natural sportsmen, 3rd grade baseball was a great place to show off their talents. For the rest of us, it was a nine inning chore, a weekly exercise in frustration, humiliation and futility.

And it was also horribly boring. I mean I'd rather have been at home watching cartoons, playing Mario, or playing with Ninja Turtles than playing, but not really *playing*, baseball on a Wednesday afternoon. Given my limited skill set (or total lack of one) I was usually placed in the spot where the ball was least likely to go. This meant the outfield, deep right field. And true enough, the ball rarely ever came my way. So, I sat down and waited. Or I searched the overgrown grass for interesting bits of trash. The few times I did come into contact with the ball often resulted in injury. I even received a concussion by colliding with the armored catcher during what was my only chance for a home run.

But back at Bundek, something has come over me. I'm mesmerized by a sport that I have actively tried to avoid for the last 25 years. Suddenly I'm watching something that just makes sense. After living in Croatia for so long, after so much confusing, awkward misunderstandings and an oscillating learning curve, here is something no one has to explain to me. I don't need a translator. I don't need to *try* and understand it. Here, there is no space for misunderstanding. Watching the players on the field, I immediately understand what is happening. I know the plays as they happen. I get it all on impulse.

I heft Sara up so she can see the game better. I try to explain to her what's happening, but she's more interested, and demanding, that we go to the big slide, and then she sees some horses someone has brought to the park... and well, baseball can't compete with horses. So we leave, but I go back a few times and watch some games. I'd go more often, but I can never find a schedule for the games at Bundek.

Despite my best attempts at conforming and transforming into a Croatian, I am, alas, still an American at heart. Turns out that I've lived in Croatia long enough to miss and like the American things I never missed or liked before, like baseball, and now American football. Just knowing that there is no American football game being watched in the homes and apartments around me on a Sunday afternoon in the Fall fills me with a vague loneliness I never would have experienced in America, because in America I didn't give a *damn* about football. The only thing to compare it to is when Croatia plays in an international sporting event, whether its football (soccer), handball, or basketball, you know that the whole country is watching it. You can hear it being broadcast all around you, feel the thrilling tension in the air even though the streets themselves are empty. It brings the nation together in an act of shared interest. To a lesser extent, the knowledge that there was a football game on television on an autumn afternoon, even if I didn't watch it, was part of an American tradition I now miss. I didn't even know America had traditions, other than you know, those holidays where we buy stuff.

So when an American-Croatian friend, who asked to be called Captain Charming Underpants in this story, called me up one January and asked if I wanted to come watch a football game at his American girlfriend's place, I jumped at the chance. Now, this game was on a Croatian sports cable channel, so it wasn't quite the same because the sportscasters were speaking Croatian, but Captain Charming Underpants, and Jane had the rudiments of an American football watching afternoon (except it was nine at night). And these include beer, tortilla chips, salsa, and some trail mix.

Most importantly, no one *hosted* anything. And I didn't have to bring a gift. Beers were in the fridge, I got one myself. That's right, I was able to open my friend's girlfriend's fridge by myself the first time I was at her house, and no one was offended! Let's take a little trip and explore some different forms of cultural etiquette. Offensive behavior varies among cultures. What some find offensive, others find normal. For example, in Japanese culture burping is considered polite. In American culture, burping at the table can get you scornful glare from grandma. In Egypt showing someone the sole of your shoe is extremely offensive, while elsewhere that's not even a thing. And in Croatia opening the refrigerator in someone else's home is considered an invasion of privacy and one of the rudest things you can do.

Who knew? Actually, I knew because this was one of the first cultural misunderstandings punica and I ever had. One summer when we were in Split, at the very beginning of my life in Croatia, punica was watching *Everyone Loves Raymond* and saw one of Ray's friends just open the refrigerator in Ray's house. My punica couldn't believe it. She called to me from the living room and stated, er... sort of asked:

"How can that guy just open the refrigerator?" I paused, trying to survey her intentions and wondering if this was a trick question.

"With... the door?"

I really didn't understand what she was asking. She elaborated, "In America, you can just go in to someone's house and open their refrigerator? Just like that?"

I stood there for a minute.

"Um... yes?" My response was met with a disconcerting head shake, that said "Tsk, tsk, tsk" with each turn.

"For us..." she didn't finish the thought, but just looked up to the heavens as if opening another's fridge was a sin so dire the offender would suffer divine retribution.

THOU SHALT NOT OPEN THY NEIGHBOR'S FRIDGE!

Now, I just thought this was my mother-in-law being a sensitive elder woman, but then I spoke with other people and there was a consensus that opening someone else's refrigerator is quite rude. And this is at complete odds to the customs of American hospitality. After all, in America we have the *Spanish* expression *Mi casa es su casa. My house is your house.* And we mean that literally as *don't ask me to get you anything or do much for you because you can just do it, get it, and eat it yourself.* Which, I guess can lead to a whole other level of rudeness in Croatia.

So back at Jane's place when I finished my beer, no one asked me if I wanted another one, I just got one on my way back from the bathroom. The most American thing about a gathering, the thing that stands in stark contrast to Croatia's custom of hospitality, is the air of casual indifference hosts have towards their guests' needs. Croatians, like Vana, might consider this rude, I consider it, *empowering!* I can get my own drinks, and when I finish one, no one insists that I have another.

I mean, I appreciate and enjoy the Croatian way of hosting, but sometimes I just need a little America to recharge my bald eagle-issue batteries. I imagine it's the same for Croatians that live abroad. They probably love going to another Croatian's home and being hosted for real, like with the pršut and cheese, and an ever-present emphasis on how you must have more, no matter how much you've had. It's probably a relief not to have to get up and get your own drinks or food.

One time I took a Croatian friend to a party in Kansas. And there the host greeted us, let us hang up our coats, and told us that there was food in the kitchen and booze in the refrigerator. *Great,* I thought and helped myself. Half an hour later I looked at my friend and realized he didn't have a drink or anything to eat. I then realized there was no way he was going to enter into someone's home for the first (or even the tenth time) and take some food from their kitchen and a beer out of their refrigerator. It just wasn't going to happen.

But it is weird to miss "American" customs and traditions in a country like Croatia that is, itself, so steeped in tradition and customs. I mean what is a traditional American food? Hamburgers? Actually, yes. No joking, that's what I miss about the US. Hamburgers, bullshit-gas-station cupcakes and fruit pies, low-rent-diner breakfasts with watered down coffee, and pie. Oh and the store Target. I miss Target, although, I did see a mysterious, plastic, shopping bag from Target, caught in the weeds by our apartment in Zagreb the other day. It's like my past is mocking me: *Here's a bag from Target— HAHAHA too bad you can't go there because you live in Europe!*

And when I literally long for not just the convenience and stuff Target offers, but the smell of a Target itself, I think, *damn,* a good part of the nostalgia I have for my homeland has been branded. When Croatians are homesick they miss the sea. When I'm homesick I miss sports I don't like, and the abundance and convenience of America. Sometimes I wonder if I've missed what America is all about, or if that's it. I mean is there more to miss? Freedom? Guns? Giant SUVs parked outside of Target?

The problem with being an immigrant is missing home, but not wanting to actually live there. So, like any immigrant group we find our fellow countrymen, carve out a space in the night and fill it with the things we think we miss from home: football, baseball, casual hosting and boardgames (but more on that later). We pretend for a few hours that we are back, but each time we get together all we really do is talk about our lives here in Croatia, because that makes for the more interesting story.

CHAPTER 11

Learning Croatian

Now lets talk about language. Croatian and English, both are intertwined in Croatia like an oddly paired couple. English is everywhere here. It's on TV, the radio, in cinemas, and even the Croatian language has incorporated English words into its vocabulary. It's not uncommon to hear people call their friend a *frendica* or to say *sorry* (more on that later). And most, if not all Croatians under the age of 50 understand English. Most people speak English, with some varying levels of success, but if they were in an emergency situation, they could survive with English. Whereas, if I were in an Emergency in Croatia, and no one spoke English, I would die (especially during my first year here).

"What's wrong?"

"Um... how do you say..." Too late. Dead.

Even though English is everywhere, any foreigner living in Croatia should learn Croatian. If you don't there will always be a distance between you and the society, and if you do... well... there will still be a distance between you and the society because Croatian is fucking hard to learn.

For a foreigner in Croatia it is very difficult to learn Croatian because usually everyone's English is better than your Croatian. And really, who wants to listen to someone murder their language when you know, they don't have to (including your Croatian wife). So many of us foreigners find ourselves locked in a vicious circle: we can't learn Croatian because no one wants to speak Croatian with us because our Croatian is so bad, but our Croatian remains bad because no one wants to speak with us. The solution, as always, is punica!

I guess all of punica's visits have helped me learn enough Croatian that I sound like I know what I am doing because at the park all the parents just speak Croatian to me. And this, this is a major step for a foreigner. Once someone starts talking to me in Croatian and keeps talking to me in Croatian, I'm often in disbelief. It's like being a teenager again, and that time I actually found a girl who thought I was attractive. I think, *Really? Are we really going to do this? Okaaaaay...* and I go with it until it ends horribly in a series of awkward utterances.

Now, when you can keep the conversation going in Croatian, that's like making it to the big leagues. SUCCESS! My biggest achievement so far has been when a Canadian friend from Istanbul visited us. At the restaurant the waiter spoke to him in English and spoke to me in Croatian! At the same table! This was like winning an Oscar for Best Performance. I'm just not sure who deserved it, me for speaking Croatian, or the waiter for going along with it. But even as my Croatian has improved there are still so many times that I'm so lost and confused that the words coming in and out turn to jumbled nonsense. And without a good grasp on the language I go back to feeling like an outsider. And worse, everyone is such a good sport about it, yet I can feel that I'm a buzzkill. I'm *Cody the Little Black Cloud, coming to rain on your fun!*

It's like I could have an animated show where I just ruin everyone's good time because I don't understand what anyone is talking about.

the Little Black Cloud

It's Cody

Croatia Strikes Back

Episode One: *The Killjoy*

"Oh boy! Some Croatian friends, I'll go talk to them…"

Me

Croatian Friends

I onda ja sam rekao…

Ha ha ha ha!

Šta ima? Zašto vi smije...err... um... what's so funny?
Oh I was just telling Goran a joke.
Can you... I mean... Možeš li mi reci?
(Sigh)

Now, now…say it in Croatian. No, no. I need to practice. Don't worry, I'll understand…

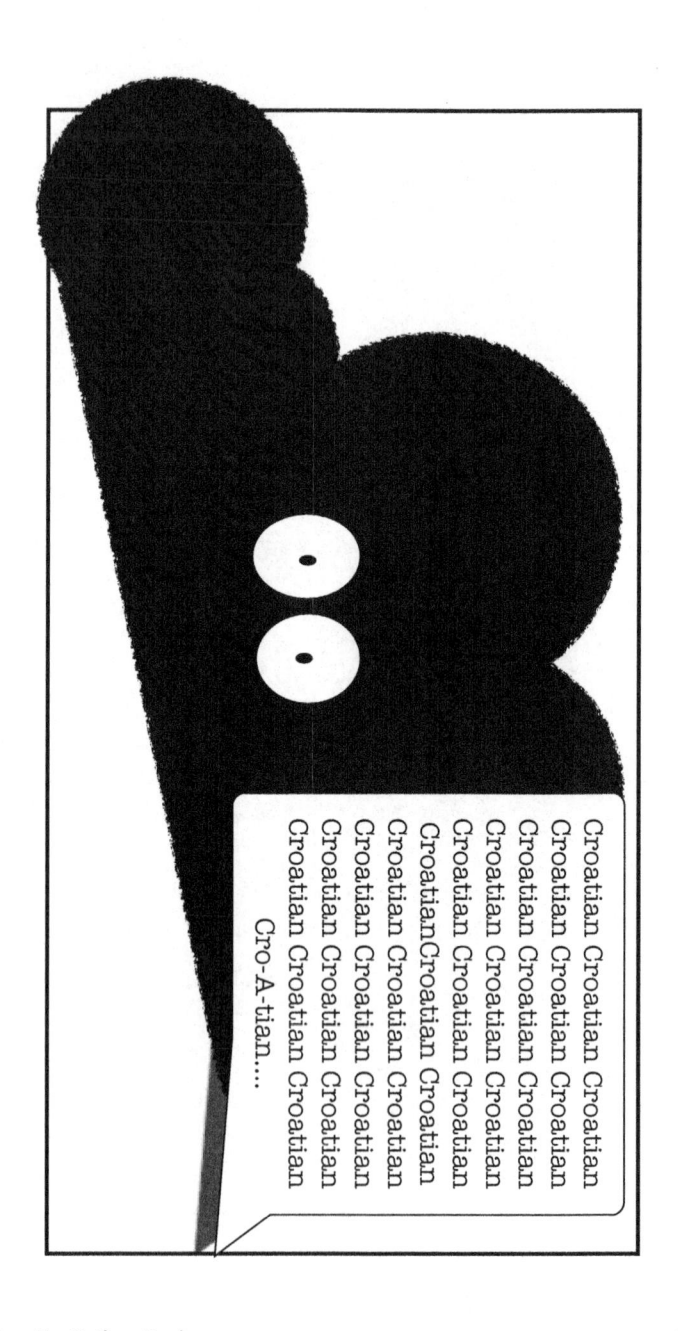

Croatian Croatian
Croatian Croatian Croatian
Croatian Croatian Croatian
Croatian Croatian Croatian
Croatian Croatian Croatian
CroatianCroatian Croatian
Croatian Croatian Croatian
Croatian Croatian Croatian
Croatian Croatian Croatian
Croatian Croatian Croatian
Croatian Croatian Croatian

Cro-A-tian....

Croatia Strikes Back

Cody McClain Brown

The worse part is when I understand all the words, but *still* don't get the joke. Having to explain a joke is like a death sentence to humor. It stops everything in its tracks and ruins a good time, just like rain on your picnic.

Croatian has so many moving parts, what with its adjective, noun case declinations and gendered verb conjugations that for non-native speakers it's like trying to unlock a combination lock, mentally solve a Rubix cube, and recite Shakespearean verse... all at the same time... while riding a bike... through heavy traffic... in the rain... at night.

But, a little bit goes a long way. A lot of Croatians are generally surprised when a foreigner speaks... *any* Croatian, let alone some with decent pronunciation. The trick is to say words like *hrvatska,* as *hRvatska* and not *HARvatska*. As an English speaker, when first learning the language I was desperately trying to stuff vowels into places they didn't belong. It was awkward, like prom night.

Speaking a little bit of Croatian has a wonderfully endearing effect on my daily encounters. I also confuse the shit out of people as I speak in a hybrid of the Dalmatian dialect and standard Croatian, poorly. In Zagreb I've left a trail of confused looks and raised eyebrows in the wake of my asking someone where the *škovace* (trash) is, or when I order *pome* (tomatoes) on my kebab. And I can never remember the standard Croatian word for fork. To me it is forever and always a *pirun*.

And how can such a small country have so many dialects? It would be like taking Texas's drawl, New Orleans specific accent (they say *oi* as *er!*), Boston's notorious *er's* and *a's*, and California's breezy slang and cram them all into... Rhode Island. Just traveling to a different region of the country can flatten my Croatian learning curve. I look on with pride (ok fine, envy too) that Sara is able to straddle her four linguistic worlds, English, Dalmatian, Zagreb-speak and Standard Croatian. The struggles of being an insider/outsider are beyond her. She flows from one world to another with the ease of a fish swimming from stormy to placid waters. More and more like a little C3PO, but with some of R2D2's attitude, she assists me as I pick her and Nora up from preschool. I tell Nora to grab her *kušin* (pillow) and she just looks at me. Blink. Pause. Blink.

"Kaj ste rekli?" She asks, the polite and Zagreb way of asking, *What the hell did you just say?*

Sara interjects: "Daddy, in Croatian Croatian we don't call it a cushion, we call it a *yastuk*."

Since Sara is bilingual and in an English group at her preschool, it is always a bigger deal for the teachers when she speaks standard Croatian rather than Dalmatian. After school the teacher tells me,

"And you know what Sara said today?"

Oh, God, what? I'm just waiting for the embarrassment. I quickly close my eyes and mutter a prayer: *Please don't let it be the F-word. Please don't be the F-word.*

"Um... What did she say?" I ask, hesitantly, already cringing inwardly. *Don't let it be the F-word.* Her teacher smiles.

"She called her socks, *čarape*, instead of *bičve*." Sara beams with pride.[6]

---

[6] *Čarape* is the standard word for socks, while *bičve* is the Dalmatian word for *socks*.

Most Croatians are very sympathetic to how foreigners struggle with their language. They really seem to appreciate the effort, any effort. Whereas in the less cosmopolitan parts of America someone struggling with English is just told: "Speak ENGLISH! WE SPEAK 'MURICAN HERE!"

Croatians are in fact much tougher on their own countrymen who don't speak English very well then they are on foreigners struggling with Croatian. In my opinion many Croatians hold themselves to a ridiculously high standard when it comes to their ability to speak English. In 2013, a Croatian politician who was an official observer in the EU Parliament famously gave a speech in which the line "People must trust us" sounded more like "Ppl mast trast as." And the country went nuts. Signs in front of cafes mocked the woman's accented English with signs reading "ppl mast dreenk caffe," memes appeared all over the internet, and views of the speech on Youtube number near a million. I can't imagine the US public ridiculing a US politician for speaking a foreign language poorly. We're just impressed when any American speaks any language other than English. *Oh, he said something in a foreign language... fancy.* Hell, we still consider JFK's famous speech in Berlin a great speech just because he spoke German. Never mind the fact that instead of declaring himself a citizen of Berlin he actually declared himself a jelly donut.

And this gets us to our second awkward episode in the life of someone learning Croatian.

Episode Two: *The Damnable Double Standard*

That moment when someone compliments you on your Croatian…

Wow. Your Croatian is really good.

Really? Um… hvala.

Unfortunately, my English isn't very good. I think it's because I don't have enough time to practice. I'm a bit lazy in that sense, you know?
!
?

Learning and speaking Croatian has many peaks and valleys. Sometimes you're up. Sometimes you're down. At times I'm amazed at the progress I've made. At other times, I'm embarrassed about how little I understand. And that can all happen while reading the same article in a daily newspaper. It's worse when you're having a conversation with someone. I present...

Episode Three: *Runaway Train: "Never coming*

Croatia Strikes Back

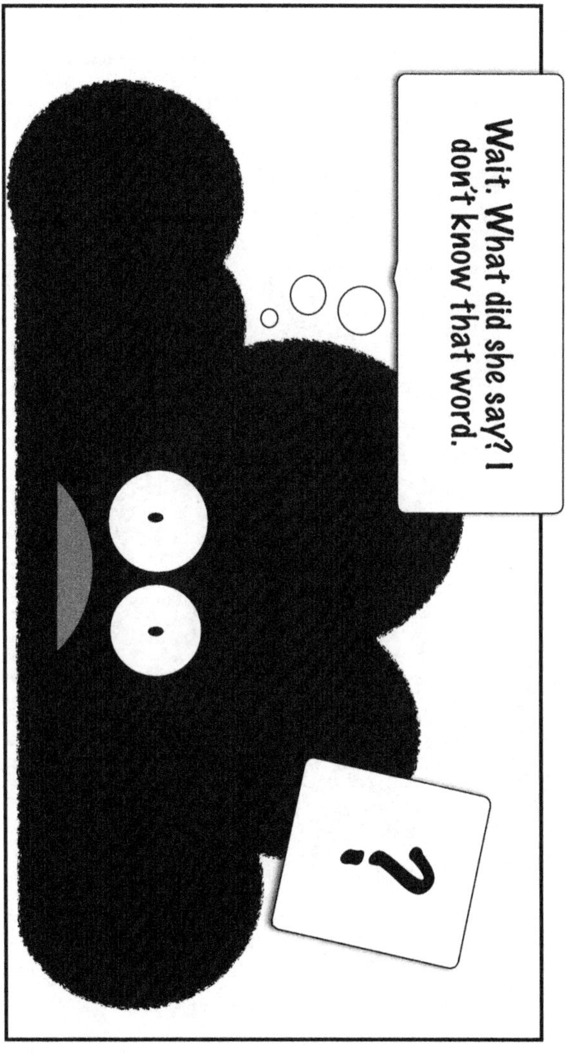
Wait. What did she say? I don't know that word.
?

And like a train running off the rails, I'm lost...

I don't any of these words either. Ah! What is she talking about? ...

And, well all right the *Adventures of Cody, the Little Black Cloud raining on everyone's Croatian fun,* might only have three episodes, but I'm afraid learning Croatian is a life-long process. Punica of course has been a huge help to me in this endeavor...

Um... rather than instruct, she just sort of yells and it's up to me to figure it out...

Molim te, utrni ga...
Utrnit? OK? She said turn it off. Now what is 'it' that she wants me to turn off?

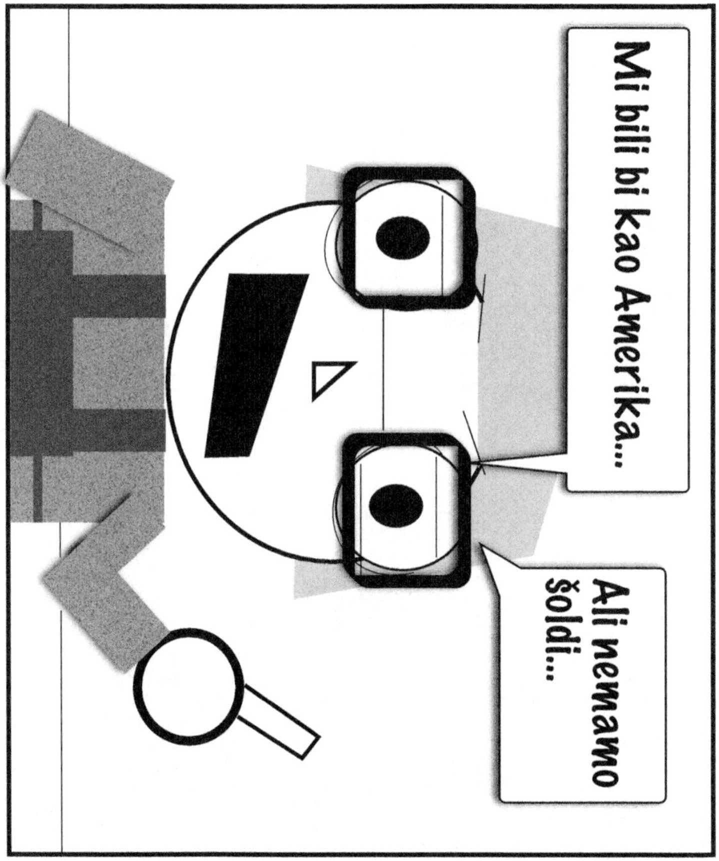
Mi bili bi kao Amerika...
Ali nemamo šoldi...

Ima puno svita tamo?

Uh... What?

Croatia Strikes Back

Language lessons with punica are punctuated with comic misunderstanding. It's either sink or swim, understand or don't. And I dare to say I think I'm finally starting to understand... all... err... most of it?

And the language lessons don't just stop with punica. As the years have gone by with Sara and her friends growing older, I often find myself correcting their English and with them correcting my Croatian.

One day Nora takes to saying, repeatedly "You are so, so, so much bad baby!" And I'm not sure what to do. Should I correct her English, explaining that she should tell me that "I'm *such* a bad baby," or tell her not to call me a "bad baby" because I'm not bad, and I'm not even a baby. Do babies have a PhD and a beard? No, they don't. Or should I just let her and Sara play video games? My reluctance to do so was what started this whole name calling affair in the first place.

And its not just Nora, all of Sara's friends try speaking English with me at various, odd times and with various results. I hear a kid's voice, that's not Sara's, yell "Come here" from the other room. Sometimes all of them sing *Let it Go*. Other times Sara's friends try saying something to me in English, giggle and then run off. As a teacher who has had to really try to get some students to overcome their self-consciousness when speaking English, I love the way Sara's friends just blurt out whatever with little hesitation. Even if that means calling me a bad baby.

And then there are their Croatian lessons. "Recite krava" (say cow) Nora demands one day. I told her I wasn't going to say "krava." A bit wounded she looked at me and said "Ali moraš učiti hrvatski" (but you must learn Croatian).

While she has a point, I'm not sure saying "krava," to a demanding six-year old is the right way to go about this.

"Do you know what krava is in English?" I ask in Croatian, I think. Nora looks at me and just yells, "COW!" before running away, laughing as if its the funniest thing in the world.

I may, at times, whine about the struggles of learning Croatian and living in a bilingual world, but when I try to imagine parenthood back home I only think about what I would be missing out on. There, we would just speak English. *Boring!* Here it's chaos. It's like painting abstract expressionism with language. In the hurried rush of commands to a gang of kids I just throw the words out, like gobs of paint on a tortured linguistic canvas, and see what sticks.

Is it frustrating at times? Sure. I mean it would be easier if I didn't have to try and urgently translate, "Don't touch the hot glue gun! I'm sorry the dog ate part of your My Little Pony! Don't go anywhere near the dog and the hot glue gun! And "No, the dog doesn't want any chocolate!"

I know that someday I'll miss the chaos and imprecision of English and Croatian in our lives. One day my daughter and her friends will be older and fluent in Croatian and English (and probably Italian and German too). One day I'll be more fluent in Croatian, and when that day comes I know I'll look back and think about the swiftness of time. I'll miss the days when they were kids and when we, me and them, all spoke so, so much like babies.

CHAPTER 12

The healthcare is (almost) free

Having coffee in Croatia often involves copious amounts of complaining. Coffee is kind of like therapy, you sit, vent, and feel better at the end. And a reoccurring theme, discussed in detail over a table laden with coffee cups, ashtrays, and small sugar packets and ignored mobile phones all over Croatia is what I refer to as the country's Institutionalized Rudeness. Yes, that's right. In Croatia we dread dealing with nearly anyone on an official level because it invariably involves the a reluctance to answer any question, no expression of regret when an answer proves wrong or inadequate, and a general terseness to any exchange. For some reason it feels as if Croatia has a special training program for bureaucratic rudeness and all bureaucrats, nurses and anyone behind a glass window really work for the Agency of Indifference and Insults.

And sure, institutions anywhere are generally unpleasant. In the US the Department of Motor Vehicles embodies everything we hate about bureaucracy. After all, this is where Homer Simpson's sister-in-law work. However in Croatia, the Institutional Rudeness stands in juxtaposition to the attitudes and behaviors people have towards one another when there exists some personal relationship. No, the air of officialdom is not impervious like a fortress of ice. Once you establish a personal relationship with someone within the system, the rudeness fades and people become overwhelming friendly (and then that produces a whole other level of awkwardness).

For example, our relationship with Sara's pediatrician and nurse. Sara's nurse is great, and nice. She inquires about how we are, engages with Sara, and takes care of our affairs with the fluid grace of a professional, which means she's quick with the stamp. Boom, Boom, Boom, she goes, stamping the document we need to get some test for Sara or a medical excuse for Sara missing school, and we're out, as quick as can be without feeling we were rushed. The whole exchange had the natural gait of an exchange among friends. Sara's doctor is equally nice, professional and responsive. The same goes for my own neighborhood nurse and doctor. The nurse even jokingly calls me "McCloud" after some cowboy detective from a show that aired long ago on TV here, which, by the way, I am totally cool with. *Cody McCloud: Cowboy Detective*.

In Croatia once you have regular, repeated interactions, you get a relationship that seems much stronger than just two people merely going about their business, doing their jobs. It's as if in Croatia, relationships are either intimate and come with the kind of warm interaction you would expect from a friend (or, like a distant cousin), or they are anonymous, and come with cold detachment. Hot or cold.

And for some reason a lot of individuals in official positions in Croatia seem to treat information like it is a form of currency, and by providing it they are somehow accruing a loss. I encountered this phenomenon the time I ended up in the hospital for five days.

Quick Digression: Someone (and we won't name names) didn't cook some chicken all the way through. I ate it out of politeness and then recommended that it be cooked a bit longer. Five days later, and I'm at the emergency room with cramping and um... stomach "issues." *Wash your hands and cook your food thoroughly people! Food born illnesses are real!* ... though my illness is still attributed by those-responsible--for-the-undercooked-chicken as the product of my poor, inadequate, American immunity, rather than to the bacteria called campylobacter, which happens to be the most commonly reported food-born illness in the European Union, infecting 190,000 people a year. No, no, it's not THAT that made me ill, it's ME *being* an American.

Anyways, aside from ascribing blame as to why I ended up in the hospital, let's return to my experience in the hospital. Croatian hospitals are certainly different than American hospitals. In the US, at least in Oklahoma, a lot of hospitals are like hotels. Each room has a bathroom, and a couple TVs (some plasma), and the rooms are air conditioned. And like most nice hotels, hospital rooms cost you A LOT of money.

Croatian hospitals, or the one I stayed in at least, on the other hand are less like hotels and more like... um... staying at summer camp. There's no TV, the windows are often open, the rooms have more people in them, and the bathroom is down the hall. Also, the parking lot at this particular hospital, which has the great name "The Hospital for Infectious Diseases," was a muddy field around the back, just like where the parents parked their cars at summer camp when they came to pick up us kids. And it turns out that if you actually *have* an infectious disease and Croatian health insurance, your stay at the infectious disease hospital is completely on the house.

But there were a few things that seemed odd. For a place that was supposed to be about rest, the nurses didn't really let me or my two roommates sleep. They came in around midnight and took our temperatures, leaving the thermometer under our arms, walking out and returning ten to twenty minutes later. Then they would do the same thing at around six or seven in the morning, loudly.[7]

All in all, the hospital had a kind of retro-aesthetics to it. It's like how I imagine a hospital from the 1960s might look, metal frame beds, three people to a room, metal utensils instead of plastic ones. As a bit of "retro" icing on the hospital's retro cake, the corridors were lined with prints of Edward Hopper paintings from the 1920s, 30s and 40s. Now, and this is just a suggestion to the hospital administration, hospitals can be lonely, depressing places. And while I appreciate good art and an institution that has good taste in art (much nicer than generic flower prints), Edward Hopper paintings might not be the way to go here. I mean art critics have described Hopper's works as "desolating pieces of realism," that capture the "lonely mood of his subject." And someone put these paintings up in a hospital? I mean it's not exactly what you want to look at as you shamble around the hospital's empty, midnight corridors, worried and wondering about your own

---

[7] Why do Croatian's take their temperature under the arm? I mean I did that as a kid, but once I was like ten or so, we always did it under our tongue. Do other countries take temperatures under the arm too? Is it the Americans that are weird?

condition, feeling the absence of your family, and contemplating the great questions of death and faith. I mean, show me a sunny sky, show me Split, or that picture of the sea and the single set of footprints on the beach with the poem about God, rather than the vacant stares of the isolated subjects in Edward Hopper's art.

Look! It's Edward Hopper's 'Automat.' I'm feeling better already!

Every day the doctor would make his rounds, sometimes with a group of medical students gathering around as he went bed by bed, looking at our charts and asking questions. And the nurses would check on me several times a day. I noticed that the younger nurses seemed nicer. Whereas, with the older nurse I felt like I had a 3 question quota for each day. I'd ask things like: "Do you think I'll be able to go home tomorrow?" Or "Could you tell me how long I'll be staying here?" Croatian hospitals seem to want to keep you in them for as long as possible. I'm sure I could have done most of my recovery from home. So, I was anxious to know how long this would all last. When I exceeded my three question quota, the nurse's answers grew more and more terse before fading altogether into an ambiguous and begrudging set of physical gestures that were clearly not answers to anything. And with the gradual deterioration of our conversation, she would leave the room.

Similar situations are repeated all over the country. When we needed to change the name on the cable and internet subscription, Vana went three times to the same guy at the cable provider, who *every time* told her it was all taken care of and would be changed in a few days. When nothing happened, she finally went to a different office and the clerk there said there was no record of anyone even ordering the changes. *Huh?* Getting adequate answers to your questions is one of life's greatest challenges in Croatia.

And I wonder if people are reluctant to divulge information because they believe it may expose some ignorance or incompetence? Or are the internal processes in this country's large firms and institutions so complicated that few people actually agree on or understand how they should and do work? Ask three people at the same job how you should file a form, process some necessary request, or whatever thing that you would assume is standardized, and you're likely to get *four* different answers.

A lot of the institutional confusion might go back to the fact that Croatia is a new country, with only 25 or so years of existence. The people working there might just not know what the process for this or that actually is. Maybe no one really knows. 25 years of transition is not that long, really. The US only got its constitution 13 years after it declared independence. Ironically, the quest for improvement creates a vicious circle. I've heard it said, or complained actually, that in order to improve the bureaucracy and these kinds of process the laws are always changing, and no one, even the workers, in some cases the people who draft the policies, are not even sure how things should *really* be done. And amid the uncertainty I think you also have the cultural idea that individuals are obligated to each other. Answering a question might be creating a personal obligation between the person making the inquiry and the person responding to it, and in a system where so much is uncertain, maybe it's best to avoid being obligated to strangers for things that are beyond your own control. Therefore clear, direct answers are best to be avoided. Part of learning to survive in Croatia is to grow less demanding for certainty and exactitude. Becoming more Croatian, I hear a voice in my head saying, come on, embrace the ambiguity! Relish in the ambivalence!

And it's not all bad. Every now and then you come across someone in officialdom who is polite, nice, and takes the time to look at you like a human, a person, someone bound up in the same hopes and fears as everyone else. And that nurse or doctor, administrator, or the very friendly lady and guy at the tax office (*really, at the TAX office? Yes!*), that person restores your faith in humanity altogether. It's like the old saying that I just made up goes: in Croatia the healthcare is free, but the smiles are priceless.

CHAPTER 13

Moving is as painful as childbirth?

If Americans move like we change socks, that is frequently, then Croatians move like people buy suits, a few in a lifetime for most. And most apartments, just like the first suit I ever owned, are inherited. Before moving to Croatia, I'd lived all over the place (four cities, three states, plus Canada, and 20 different houses and apartments, not to mention two years and two apartments in Istanbul). Any my wandering wasn't a generational young man's game, in the last decade my mom and step-dad, dad and step-mom have all moved to new houses, my sisters have each moved to a different place, and my brother has changed apartments several times. In America, we really do change residency like we change socks. I guess, the remnants of the past's pioneering spirit haunts our present, turning us into spectral vagabonds.

And while Americans posses a very nomadic soul, we are tied to nowhere for very long, Croatians are much more sedentary, they live and belong to a place in ways that are hard for me (and most Americans) to understand. Like a ring of concentric circles there is a bond, an attachment to their apartment, their street, their neighborhood, and then their city or town. Look at the pride people take in being a "real Purger" (Zagreb native of at least three generations) or a "real Splićanin" (a person from Split for a LOT of generations). I've never met an Oklahoman proud of his generations of living in Oklahoma: 1) because it's Oklahoma; and 2) most Oklahomans, save for the Native Americans, haven't lived there for generations and even most of Indians came from somewhere else. Maybe you get a sense of this pride from the older residents of New York or some other east coast metropolis, old-timers who can remember when their neighborhoods had their own character and culture. But, out on the ranges of the West we have more pride in our mobility than in our ability to stay in a place for any length of time, let alone for three or four generations.

I was coming to learn that when trying to sell or buy an apartment in Croatia, one of the hardest things, much harder than negotiating a price, was for the owner to break that bond with their apartment, neighbors, and neighborhood. Or at least that's the only way I can explain what kept happening to us.

After seeing our dream apartment we decided to make an offer, never mind the place's legal issues and impossible, Escher-esque physics. First, I made an offer. And just like my attempt in trying to find a prom date in 1997, I wasn't rejected out right. There was hope! However, and just like prom, a few days later the owner found a better offer. He called, saying that the apartment had sold. Except... about three months later the owner called us back, explaining that the deal had fallen through and he was interested in our offer. And like a bad romance, we'd become trapped in an on again off again relationship with an apartment?

For the next month we poured over documents, the building and the apartment's original plan, trying to determine where the changes had been made, and wondering what the consequences of those changes might mean to us later on. Since it seemed like everyone, everywhere had made "illegal" changes to their place, we weren't that worried about it.

We scoured the poorly xeroxed pages, comparing them to more recent plans. We met with our friend Vesna, Mirko's wife and Nora's mother, who was also a lawyer. We asked her what she thought. And she thought:

"Don't buy this apartment." And Vesna is a very determined woman. Partially deaf she managed to complete one of the most difficult Colleges in the University of Zagreb's system, the College of Law. As a lecturer at the College of Political Science, many of my students are refugees who washed out of the law school and washed up on our shores. And they are good students, so to finish the College of Law in any case, let alone with an any kind of impairment is no easy task.

Vesna carried in her manner an air of determination and the will of a freight train. You did not want to get in her way. You could see in her defiant demeanor that she had spent her youth growing up in Yugoslavia and later Croatia, fighting against what other's thought she could and couldn't do, daring to defy the boundaries of other's expectations. To go against her advice is no easy endeavor, and the fact that we were willing to, shows just how much we *wanted* this apartment.

We were too mentally and emotionally invested at this point. I was confident in my American fueled optimism that everything would work out and that Vesna, well Vesna was just taking the typical, skeptical, pessimistic Croatian view. *Fine,* was Vesna's attitude, but she insisted on one thing. And I mean really insisted on it. Bound up in her advice was all the uncertainty of the Croatian judicial and legal system, wrapped in the duty of her friendship to us. None of which in Croatia are to be ever taken lightly.

Over coffee while Nora and Sara played in the park Vesna asked us,

"Was the apartment's owner married?"

"Yes," Vana replied.

"Did they buy the apartment when they were married?"

"Yes," I replied.

"But now they are divorced, right?"

"Yes, but what does this have to…" Vesna cut me off with a look. She locked eyes with both me and Vana, her steely gaze hardened by both determination and personal concern. It said that we could dismiss some of her advice, but that if we dismissed what she was saying now she would no longer be our friend and would stop giving us advice. She might even murder us for being too dumb to live.[8] Such was her understanding of her obligation to us as a friend, she had a responsibility to keep us from acting stupid. The hairs on my arm stood on end.

---

8 I let the "real" Vesna read this part to see if she had any issues with what I wrote about her. The only thing that bothered her was me writing that she would stop being our friend. She wanted to make sure that we knew that that wasn't true. And I guess it wasn't, but that look in her eye… we'll just say I added that last part for dramatic effect. And notice how she didn't say the part about killing us was wrong, just that she would have still been our friend. Such is the strength of Croatian friendship. Even in a story it has no limits, it extends through murder, and even endures beyond the grave.

Cody McClain Brown

"Make sure he gets his ex wife to sign a declaration that she will not make a claim on the apartment." *Wait? What?* I didn't understand. Why would we need that? They are already divorced. *Aha!* This is Croatia... where apparently getting divorced "officially" dissolves your marriage, but does nothing to resolve the couple's jointly owned property. So we've come full circle, we are back to property being one of the main, if not the main, problems in Croatia. I don't know how it is in other countries, but divorce in the US is ALL ABOUT PROPERTY! I remember in the aftermath of my parents' divorce, and the divorce of my friends' parents (hey it was the 1980s, everyone got divorced), property was discussed and divided. My mom got the house, my friend's dad got their old house, my other friend's mother got the house until he turned 18 (and until that time she did nothing to repair it, it stood rotting in the neighborhood like Miss Havisham's wedding cake). Someone always "got" something and the words were spoken with such finality (and often vehemence) that you knew it was permanent.

In Croatia, nope, none of that. And if we didn't get this declaration from the owner's ex, then, apparently, she could show up at anytime and claim to own half of the apartment, and we would be responsible for buying her out, even though we'd bought the apartment from the actual owner. Anything purchased or earned in Croatia while married is jointly owned by the couple, but can be left as an outstanding issue even after the divorce.

"Well sure," we said to Vesna, "We will get him to get his ex wife to sign a document." I mean, how could that be a problem, they're divorced, he's selling the apartment. Well... after months of dealing with all the other paperwork, after the first offer, the failed sale, the new agreement, and everything else, the owner refused to ask his ex to sign this document. We were disappointed. Amid our devastation, like survivors trying to salvage something from the rubble, we still hoped for a way around this:

"But maybe we could…"

"No." Vesna exclaimed with the quiet force of a looming storm.

"Or we could…"

"No." Thunder rolled in Vesna's eyes. I exhaled. Like the air leaving my body, my dreams floated into the emptiness of the world around us. Vana tried again with the owner, explaining clearly that without that document, we would not buy the apartment. Still, he refused. And so we walked, back into the Quixotic fray, searching for an apartment.

A few months later we found one that was "all right." A bit smaller, but in a newer building and with no outstanding physics-bending-legal issues, and the owner had even read my book! The problem was that the price was high. We offered what we could afford and after a few weeks, we met with the owner and her realtor. She accepted our offer, but said that first she would have to find a place to move in to. We were fine with that as we weren't really in a hurry. So we parted, Vana and I celebrated with a neighbor visiting from Split, and we thought we had done it. We were buying an apartment! HOOORAH!

But (and you just knew that was coming), the owner kept showing the apartment to other people. *Wait? What?* We called the agent asking if we still had a deal, even offering a deposit. The agent replied that the owner was still hoping for a better deal, but that yes we did have a deal, but maybe we should keep looking for an apartment ourselves. *Huh?* So, the deal "we had," wasn't really a deal.

Now, after these two events where we had agreed on a price, and we were ready to buy the apartment, we had two owners who basically didn't really seem to want to sell. One thing to know is that at this time (and probably still) the Zagreb real-estate market was horrible. Apartments sat and lingered on the market for years. Very few people were buying. Therefore, to have someone, like ourselves, agree to buy an apartment was something that shouldn't have been taken lightly. And in both cases we had negotiated and agreed on the price, and yet, no sale. Moving in Croatia, it just ain't easy.

And here is why. I mean look at us, Mrs. Dalmatia and Mr. America, who we were determined to stay in a specific neighborhood in Zagreb? *Wait? What?* American-me would never even blink at the idea of moving to the other side of the city. But, Croatian-me? Ha, Croatian-me was kept up at night at the thought of moving just a kilometer east. Why? Because that's how it works. Once you lay down some roots in some plot of Croatian soil, it's hard to dig them out.

As frustrated as I was at the last two owners, I was beginning to understand. I'd lived in Vrbik for just four years, and yet the idea of moving terrified me. Partly, because it feels permanent. In the US, you just think, *Well, if I don't like it here, I'll just move*. I mean, that's apparently what all my ancestors did. But, even after just four years in Croatia, I'd begun to feel and notice something different. Places aren't just spaces, they are something more than that. And if I was reluctant to change neighborhoods after *only* four years, how does it feel to move for someone who has lived in the same apartment, and the same neighborhood for the last 20 or even 40 years? Moving might literally feel like an impossibility.

And then, just as it looked darkest, Vana found an apartment that was *too* good to be true. It met all of our requirements and then some. It was in Vrbik. It was near Sara's school. It was also the same building that Sara's two best friends lived in, and whose parents happened to be our closest friends in the neighborhood, Adrian and Marta, Mirko and Vesna. And it was even on the side of the building that we preferred, with a wonderful, functional layout, and a terrific view of Zagreb.

And yes, it was *waaaaaay* out of our budget. In a masochistic act we went to look at the apartment anyway. While walking through the halls and in the rooms, we noticed that it wasn't completely redone like the ad had said. In fact it had some "issues," but at the same time, it wasn't in ruins like so many of the other apartments we'd seen. This gave us hope. Maybe we could get the owner to go down on the price, and then repair it piecemeal.

A few days later, Vana made an offer (because it was in Croatian). The owner of course said it was too low. Dang. Then, a Christmas miracle! (Even though this was in February). She called us back and said after talking to her sons, we might be able to come to a deal. A week later we met and agreed on a price…

… And then went to this bank, that bank, and many other banks. Even with our life savings, and our frugal nature (i.e., Vana tends to wear clothes like she's waiting for them to come back into style… and then, they do!) we still needed a ginormous loan from a bank. We finally found one that would give us a loan at an interest rate we could afford, in kuna, because I'm not going to get a loan in a currency I'm not paid in, for the next, oh, say 30 years. And the jokes on them because who knows what the hell the world is gonna look like in 30 years!?! I imagine making our last loan payment to a consortium of Chinese-Martian-American-German companies who one the Second Bank of Jupiter or something. Or maybe we'll be in debt to some kind of sentient robots overlords run by Facebook or Google. *Here you go Robot overlords, our last loan payment. Remember when I used to think you all were only good for helping me spread the word about my blog? All Hail the Great Google-Face! All Hail the Great Google-Face!*

… anyway, FIVE MONTHS later, we moved in.

Moving in Croatia is about more than changing locations or spaces. In the days of European exploration America became the New World, and Europe the Old. If there was ever a way in which I could come to fully understand what this conception means, it is embodied in the emotions and feelings of moving. The attachment I've witnessed among all the people attempting to sell their apartments, and the difficulty we ourselves had in letting go of where we lived, is evidence that a greater relationship to place and people exists in Croatia than anyplace I've lived in the US. And this is perhaps why it is so much harder for families and individuals to deal with the Croatian reality that large segments of each generation must move abroad. It is a connection that I have trouble understanding, but I have begun to feel myself (maybe it's just better to call it magic?).

On the last day, when everything had been signed and stamped (how many stamps? Oh about a baazzilion), it seemed as if the owner of the apartment wasn't really ready to move. She took a moment to tearfully collect herself. Part of me felt as if I were a Trump-like real-estate developer in some 1980s movie, like *The Goonies*, evicting an older woman from her apartment. *Just sign the papers! Mwahahahahaha! Tremendous.* Even after having the apartment on the market for over a year, even after all the paperwork and hurdles we'd had to cross to get to this point, the reality of moving seem to remain an impossibility.

The apartment had been her father's, and then hers. It was passed on through generations like a family heirloom, just, you know a very *large* heirloom. Her sons had grown up there and then, due to the economic situation in Croatia, moved abroad like so many others. They didn't want to return, and so that's why she was selling it.

After we moved in, I even felt a bite of the past, gnawing at me, as if it still wasn't "our" place. In a way it felt more like an awkward inheritance than a transaction. Something seemed to be missing. The owner had generously left some armoires in the house. One of them was in what-would-be Sara's room. When I opened it, I saw that the doors were covered in old stickers. I called Vana, she came in and was shocked. She smiled. She knew exactly what the stickers were and that they were from the 1980s. Some came from a German magazine that was popular in Yugoslavia called *Bravo*, like the pictures of the pop stars Nena (*99 Luftballons*) and Limahl (NeverEnding Storyyyyyyy, Ah ah ah aah), and some stickers of nude cartoon characters that say in Croatian, *Ljubav je...* ("Love is..."). Apparently, these were things kids collected? There were even some He-Man stickers that I remembered having when I was a kid in America. Though the colors were a little off, so they might've been counterfeit Yugoslav stickers. What does socialist He-Man say? *I, and the proletariat have the power?*

But here in this old armoire they'd been preserved like insects in amber. There was a feeling that these stickers were artifacts in an archeological find. In a way it felt right, as if our present occupation of the apartment was linked to the past of the previous occupants. Vana, or I for that matter, could have easily stuck these stickers in this cabinet when we were kids. It was like we'd opened a hidden door to Vana's and my childhood. And somehow, this link blessed the passing of the apartment from one family, one life, to our family and our life. And that's what moving in Croatia feels like, less like an investment, a function of market forces, and more like a rite of succession, a ritual of inheritance.

So, we bought an apartment! A bit anti-climatic right? I mean, I bet you thought this was going to be the last scene in the book: Us getting the keys and me lifting Vana over the threshold, ready to live the Croatian-American dream! Ha! I can't lift Vana, she's taller than me. No, the Croatian bureaucracy and the challenges of just getting someone to sell us their apartment killed all the joy and sense of triumph that you thought (and I thought) might come with finally buying our ideal apartment. At one point in the long process Vana remarked: "I hope this is like childbirth, painful, but eventually you forget about that because afterward you get a baby." I just cast a side-long glance at her unsure what to say. Turns out, moving in Croatia IS LIKE CHILDBIRTH, painful, but in the end you get an apartment... and a mortgage! In a way it's a lot like having a kid. You hope you'll love it forever, because that's how long you'll be paying for it.

"Love is..." a couple of stickers I still don't understand

CHAPTER 14

Bureaucracy! The never ending nightmare

So, you want to buy an apartment? And Croatia is all like:

```
......................./~/)
....................,/~./
.................../..../
............./~/'...'/~`.,
........./'/.../.../......./~\
......('(...´...´....⁻~/'...')
.........\................,'..../
..........''...\..........._.´
...........\..............(
.............\..............\...
```

Croatians and myself can't believe the energy spent on getting the paperwork just right so that you can finally purchase an apartment or anything in this country. When my friend Captain Charming Underpants traded his old car to a friend for some books and a couple board games (really it was kind of a favor), it took a month to get the paperwork in order. Now, imagine what it must take to buy an apartment? I'm told that if we'd used a realtor we wouldn't have had quite this many bureaucratic entanglements, but I'm skeptical (Hey! Look's whose becoming more and more Croatian).

Here is a list of all the government and private institutions, offices or agencies, myself, Vana, or the apartment's owner had to visit, and the number of times we had to visit each one, before we could close on the sale.

Department of deeds	6
Tax office	5
Ministry of Defense	3
Ministry of the Interior	5
US Embassy	1
Public Notary	4
Accounting office at University of	3
Accounting office at Vana's work	4
Bank	10
Total	41

And what does each visit to each of these places consist of? Basically, taking a stamped document from one place and getting another one from another place because in

Croatia, bureaucracies don't talk to each other. Seriously, the Ministry of the Interior, you know the place in charge of ID's and official addresses, my resident permit, was, until recently, unconnected to the country's 428 municipal departments that keep track of marriages, births, deaths and all kinds of other stuff. So each time I had to report for my annual I'm-still-in-Croatia-update I had to get a copy of my marriage certificate from Split that was no more than three months old in order to show the Ministry of the Interior that I was still married. And that was really fun because I live in Zagreb. So each year my mother-in-law went and waited at Split's municipal office, got a copy of my marriage certificate and then mailed it to us in Zagreb. And that's just one example. As one friend put it, "Croatian bureaucracy has a paper fetish."

When a group of American university students came to Croatia one summer, we visited a very prominent international organization, that... um... let's just say is like a "global" bank. We spoke to its president and during a Q and A session, and when I asked him what the "bank" saw as the biggest problem in Croatia, he said the biggest problem Croatia faced was attracting foreign investment and getting the economy to grow. And that the source of this problem wasn't the Croatian "mentality" or any broader conceptual problem (that many people here like to blame the Croatia's problems on), rather it was simply the country's bureaucratic inefficiencies and redundancies.

"And the oddest thing," he went on, "is that everyone in government knows this." He explained that after working in countries like Indonesia and Turkey, Croatia was the only country where everyone agreed with his organization's critiques. When he or the representatives of this organization met with Government ministers, they would all say, "Yes, you're right." But no one knew how to change any of it.

Along with the hassle of having to visit each office multiple times and wait in multiple lines comes the fact that everything about the process is opaque. Like... it's on purpose. *Why do we need this document?* You never really know. *How long will it take to get?* No one has any idea. The amount of time involved in submitting a document for approval and then getting it back with the accompanying document that you need to then take to another department ranges from a week to... *forever?*

We were lucky. *Really?* No, really. The longest we had to wait for one document was a month. Of course we didn't know how long it would be, and the wait kept forcing us to revise our plans to move out from our rented apartment on the 1st, to the 15th, to the 1st of the following month. And while we waited for this particular document, Vana kept calling the department that the woman selling us her apartment had taken it to.

Now, here is the really weird thing, I had expected all of this to be an impenetrable process in which we had no one to talk to. I imagined that once you submitted the document it then just vanished into some kind of document nether world, like a limbo for documents. Each document floats in the ether, moaning and wailing, until the Wise Sages of the Bureaucracy used their magic to summon one back to the land of the living for the stamping ceremony. Boom, ink, boom, and your document is saved!

But it wasn't like that all. There was no magic, and surprisingly little mystery.

Vana was able to actually call and talk to a woman in the department where we'd sent the document, and like asking about the condition of a patient, she was able to ask about our document's status. Turns out this made the whole affair even more frustrating because for two weeks she learned that everything concerning the document and whatever it was supposed to do had been approved, BUT the head of the department had failed to sign the document. So, here Vana is on the phone, explaining the urgency, i.e., we told our landlord we would be out on the 1st, maybe somebody is planning to move in that day or the next day, and all the document needs is the signature of someone whose job it is, presumably, to sign such documents and... so? *Right. I understand, but she hasn't signed the document yet? No. Madame, the document will be signed when the head of the department signs it.*

And then, when the document was finally signed, it had to go to a public notary. Actually it had to go to THE public notary because this particular state agency only used one. And that one was apparently far away because the woman in the office kept explaining how her assistant had to take all the documents, once they were signed (and who knows when that would be) by tram to THE public notary. After the document was notarized by the public notary, whom Vana was also able to call and ask for an update, then the documents would wait until the assistant returned and brought all of them back to the department... by tram. Vana asked if she could pick it up. *No.* And deliver it to the department ourselves? *No.* So, we waited, postponing our move twice and we were fortunate enough that the apartment we were living in hadn't been rented to a new tenant in the meantime.

Now, go back and look at that table I made. Take all those agencies and multiply the uncertainty and the waiting by like a billion and you can get a sense of how this process just gnaws and gnaws on your nerves.

And then finally we had all the documents and stamps! Now we could buy the apartment! And that involved making a sizable down payment in cash, which is no problem because we'll just take our entire, once in a lifetime, lifesavings out from the bank and put it in a bag and walk to the public notary's office? *Wait? What? Th-thats a lot of money to be walking around with.* But in Croatia, entirely normal!

For weeks I had been fretting about making the cash down payment on the apartment. All our money was tied up in three different currencies. I frantically watched the exchange rates of the dollar, kuna and euro rise and fall. When we had calculated whether or not we could even buy this apartment the dollar had been much stronger to the euro, but of course that had been long before we'd began our arduous bureaucratic odyssey. Now, the dollar was weaker to the euro. At night I laid in bed fearing a global economic crisis occurring the day before we were supposed to purchase the apartment. Something like Brexit, where the British pound fell by 17% in one day! Maybe a financial bubble was waiting to burst a couple days before we were to purchase our apartment. Such an event would send the price of our apartment soaring and leave us short, and screwed as we would lose our deposit because we wouldn't be able to afford the apartment or we would wind up in a long and protracted legal dispute.

And that was just one of my worries. The other concern was the fact that the apartment's owner wanted us to pay her in cash. Not through a bank transfer, not through a check or money order (because I don't think those last two things exist in Croatia), but cash. Which meant we had to carry the money out of the bank where it was safely stored, and insured, and to the exchange office (which gave us a better rate than the bank) and then give it to the owner, at the Signing of the Contracts for the apartment.

Now, in the US you just don't walk around with large sums of money, unless you are a drug dealer (or a lobbyist, *amlright?*). I know people who have *literally* (and I mean that in real sense of the word) been robbed walking down the street, into a store, or to their car, at night or in broad daylight. Though the odds are remote, there are still odds that you might be robbed if you walk around, carrying your entire life savings.

Meanwhile in Croatia, well, this is apparently not a problem. I finally accepted it and thought, *Well, OK. Vana and I will go together. Strength and safety in numbers.* I was nervous because we also had to contact the exchange office the day before and order the money. Now, what's to stop them from tipping off some thieves that some dumbasses are coming by with a bunch of money? We could walk out of the office, walk a block and WHAMO! Get robbed. And then there would be nothing we could do about it. Our money, our apartment, our dreams gone in an instant of violence. If there was ever a point when my American need for a firearm was tingling, it was now. Was I paranoid? Probably, but nevertheless, I wanted to be paranoid and armed. *AMERICA!*

So it was planned. We had a date. We had a time. We were going to exchange the currency and make the down payment. Except, a couple days before it's all set to go down, Sara woke up with chicken pox (and yes American parents, I know about the vaccine). *Can you believe it?* Worst of all, we had no punica this time (she was in Split), and therefore someone had to stay home with her. Me!

So, I'm stuck at home while Vana is out there, in the wilds of Zagreb, walking the city streets with tens of thousands of Kuna in her purse. Our entire, once-in-a-lifetime, life savings. I gaze out the window in a state of fretful anxiety. If I had a cigarette I would smoke it. Then something draws my attention. Some music. I look at the TV and see *Blaze and Monster Machines* is starting. I look at the couch and there's Sara, her face dappled in red, scabby dots, her eyes moving between me and the TV.

"Daddy, what's wrong?"

"Nothing, sweety," I say and sit down next to her. For the next twenty minutes I watch a show about talking monster trucks, who for some reason still have drivers even though they are apparently living, sentient beings. Like are they just talking, thinking heads who can't control their own bodies? Weird, right? And they also do math problems through the course of their adventures. This was never how I imagined today would go.

After the cartoon, I begin pacing the room nervously, glancing out the window, looking at my phone, hoping the worst was just in my over-active American imagination.

At last the phone rings.

Vana tells me the down payment, the currency exchange, and the signing of the contracts all occurred without a problem because God damn, if there is one thing Croatia has it is safety. And the craziest part to me (and probably most Americans), was that the owner, who is in her 60s, just took the money, stuck it in her purse and continued to run errands, walking around the city with hundreds of thousands of kuna just in her bag.

Croatia: where even the idea of robbing little old ladies... evidently doesn't exist.

But after all that, after such an exhausting process, marking off each item from the list of frustrating things, while still not knowing if the list was actually complete, there was no triumphant entrance into our new place. Instead we sort of cautiously, emotionally, crept inside, waiting, watching for some other obstacle to emerge of our nowhere like a cloaked highwayman standing ominously in the distance on a dark and lonely road.

Oh but wait! We're not done. Ha-ha, fooled you. You thought this chapter about bureaucracy was over... it's never over... never!

After we bought the apartment we had to change our address at, um... every place that has our old address, but first we had to get our official I.D.s

So, for about a month we had to continue to use our old mailbox in our old building. In the US, and I imagine elsewhere, you can provide the post office with a forwarding address, until everything is officially changed... not in Croatia. At the same time Sara was now old enough that she needs an official I.D. So we register for that too. And another odd quirk about getting your kid's I.D. is that one parent has to apply for the I.D. and the other parent has to pick it up. I don't know what they do if there isn't another parent.

So three weeks after moving, I go to MUP (the Ministry of the Interior) early one morning, wait in line for my I.D. at the foreigner section and then I try to pick up Sara's I.D. The only problem is I don't know where to go for Croatian I.D.'s. It's not the same desk as for foreigners. All the signs and everything are written in OFFICIAL Croatian, which involves words you only hear when you need to do the official thing that you need to do. I mean, most of the time that I speak Croatian it involves me talking about lunch and coffee. Getting I.D.'s has never been a point of conversation. Lost, I return to the machine that dispenses the numbers you need to wait in line, press the button for English (*Hey! There is one! All right!*), and try to figure out from the translations which section I need to visit to get Sara's I.D.

And while I'm there slowly trying to decipher what's what and where's where, a line begins to form. Yes, that's right. We now have a line for the thing that gives you a number to get in line. And I'm the cause of it. *Great.* It grows longer and longer, and finally people begin to "offer," more like insist because I'm taking so damn long, their help. I try to explain what I need and everyone is saying,

"Here, you have to go the foreigner desk."

"But, it's not for me. It's for my girl!" Now here I just make things worse and more confusing. In Croatian I make the mistake and say *cura*, which means girl, but is usually used as girlfriend, when what I should have said was *curica*, which means little girl and is taken as daughter. So, everyone assumes that I need an I.D. for my girlfriend who must also be foreign because otherwise wouldn't she come and do this incredibly complicated language lesson herself?

And one of the other little quirks about the people going to the "foreign" section at the Ministry of the Interior, the mass of humanity that has collapsed from a line behind me to a pressing crowd of "helpful" individuals, is that they are mostly from Bosnia and Herzegovina, so they all understand and speak Croatian. So, there I am, trying to find the right place to go to pick up my Croatian daughter's I.D., while trying to convince a bunch of native speaking "foreigners" that I, the clearly foreign guy, AM NOT looking for the section for foreigners! Eventually, I flee to the nearby McDonalds, wrapping myself in the therapeutic, calming scents and tastes of "home" (did I seriously just write that about McDonalds? Sigh) and call Vana. I plead for her to leave work and come help me. Of course I still have to be there because I am the other parent designated to pick up Sara's I.D., which is why we sent me in the first place. Vana arrives and an hour and a half later, our number is finally called. We approach the window, and sure enough, the lady will only give the I.D. to me, because I'm not the parent who dropped off the original application.

And with that all the paper work was over, we were done. We'd finally moved in.

Or had we...

CHAPTER 15

The biggest difference between here and there

But hey! We had moved! We were in an apartment that every day seemed more and more perfect for us! And the best part was we hadn't had to leave our neighborhood, Vrbik. Positioned near the crossroads of two of Zagreb's most vital streets, Savska and Vukovarska, Vrbik is close enough to be near the center, but far enough away to feel peaceful and a bit suburban.

In the last book I said I would live in Vrbik forever (*4 life bitches*, is actually what I wrote), and now it seemed that was actually true… because once you buy an apartment in Croatia A) selling it seems unlikely given the market; and B) who in their right mind wants to go through all that again! So, Vrbik it was, and is, "til death do us part."

Vrbik feels like a village, and I don't mean that in the pejorative sense, but in the communal sense. Most everyone here "knows" each other. Maybe I don't know the name of that guy walking his dog, but I *know* that guy and I *know* the dog. Maybe I don't know the name of the older gentleman I would see making his way to the bakery every morning, just as I took Sara to preschool, but I know I'll see him tomorrow (Fun fact: turns out this guy that I saw literally every time I took Sara to preschool, is now our neighbor. He even lives on the same floor we just moved on to!) And there is something to be said for all this familiarity. In our fair village of Vrbik, nestled in the heart of Zagreb's metropolis, acquaintance fosters concern and concern creates a community.

The strength of a neighborhood's community in Croatia, its pulses and rhythm, is apparent throughout Croatia, beyond our neighborhood in Zagreb. In Split it was evident, I mean in the last book I have a whole chapter about my punica's neighbors. And while in American neighborhoods, especially those in the suburbs where the neighbor association has rules governing what you can and cannot do to your house and lawn, there are no such rules outside my punica's apartment in Split. The value of community may cost the aesthetic pleasantries we so adore in the US.

Each night the old neighbors sit like the three Fates. They appear to be all knowing, spinning yarns about everything and everyone. Three hunched shadows, silhouetted against the street light, they sit on a bench, the ends of their cigarettes flaring and fading in the evening's shadows. Their conversation murmurs through the apartment block's open windows like some dull television sounds in an adjacent room.

The bench is not really a bench, but a collection of chairs scattered around a table set on the lawn in front of the apartment block. There is a bench, but it is incidental to the chairs. Of course the chairs aren't a single set like you would buy at the store. Rather, each chair is unique, each with its own mysterious origin. Somehow each one just showed up, sprouting around the bench like a bunch of mushrooms.

The three old neighbors serve as the core of the group. Others come and go, but the orbit of the evening belongs to these old women. They are my mother-in-law's neighbors. The women who watched my wife grow up and now kiss and hug my daughter in the hallway, passing her treats or just bringing up plates of crepes for no reason in the evening.

Some people, mostly guys, make fun of the idea of old ladies gossiping on the country's benches. In Croatia it seems like every neighborhood has their set of the Fates, their group of neighbors who congregate nightly. Sometimes, they're considered nosy, judgmental, and the source from which so many rumors spring. "Did you hear about…" "I heard that…" "No, she said he said…"

But for me, when I sit and envision the loneliness of the American midwest, when I recall how easy it is to become lost in our culture of individual isolation, then I think everyone would appreciate the ladies on the bench. After living in Paris for ten years in the 1930s, the author Henry Miller returned to the US and wrote a book called *The Air Conditioned Nightmare* in which he expressed how utterly isolated Americans seemed from each other and nature. I have to agree with him. Once air conditioning was invented we no longer had to go outside to keep cool during the hellish summer months. So we saw our neighbors less and less. Add to this equation the advent of the television age and we no longer needed company. So, there was no need to see our neighbors at all. Now, to see someone its like you need an excuse to intrude on their solitude.

But during my early months in Croatia, when we spent the whole summer in Split I knew that whenever I came or went, I'd see the neighbors on their "bench." And it goes on today, I'll stroll up or park the car, catching their squints in the flash of the headlights, and even if I don't want to, I'm drawn to walk over and at least say hi.

We make jokes, I mention propuh, they ask about my daughter. If my wife, daughter and I have been out together then usually my mother-in-law is down there waiting for us with them. Maybe she'll take my daughter upstairs, and my wife and I will steal a cigarette and a few minutes with the neighbors.

Amid the manicured front lawns of America's McMansions, the long driveways and wide streets, there is no place for a bench, let alone a sordid collection of mismatched, broken lawn chairs. What serves as the center of the community in Split, Croatia would be seen as a property devaluing eyesore in Oklahoma. And that might be the difference between here and there. Property over community, value over spirit. But, after living in Croatia I say let the old ladies talk on the bench. I see that in the end, we're richer for it.

And in Vrbik there are benches, cafes, and a geography populated with familiar faces of friends and acquaintances. I imagine the same is true of most neighborhoods throughout Croatia, which I suppose, helps explain why it's so difficult to move. Unlike in America where moving from one side of the city is nothing, in Croatia it's not just apartments you're changing, it's more than a familiar building you're leaving, it's the whole community.

In Vrbik we had our friends, Mirko and Vesna with their daughter Nora, Adrian and Marta with their daughter Sonja. When we seriously considered moving to another neighborhood, they all seemed to imply that though our friendships would endure, it could never be the same as it was with us living in the same neighborhood. A short time earlier Mirko and Vesna had seriously considered moving abroad, but had remained. At one point while we deliberated about an apartment 2 kilometers from where we were currently living, Vesna reminded Vana that "after all they hadn't moved to Dubai." That's right, changing neighborhoods in Croatia can be considered the same as moving to the Middle East.

Maybe it's because we were no longer renters, but homeowners (excluding the fact that the bank *really* owned our apartment), but I felt as if the community in the building we'd just moved into, though bigger, was also more involved. Where as in America I was used to living in buildings with strangers, I could tell that the people in this building were intimately involved with each other. Immediately, as we were moving in and I was waiting for the elevator with a load of boxes, the building's residents began coming up to me.

A few began "introducing" themselves in a way that felt like an interrogation. *Who are you? Where are you from? Which apartment are you moving in to? Is it the one from the guy that died? No? Oh it's the one from the lady moving to the sea? Did you get a good price? How much? Just tell me per square meter? Is it in good shape? Does it have a security door? Security door! Does it have one?*

"Um… nice to meet you?" Usually in these moments I pretend I can't understand what someone is saying. But this time I wanted to make a good impression so I tried to be as specifically vague as possible.

"We got a good price, but the place needs some work." Or,

"It's a good size, much bigger than our older, 72 square meter apartment." And when that failed to assuage the barrage of questions,

"Sorry, I'm an American. I don't understand Croatian."

And I was fine with this, really. I was and am happy to know that everyone here knows who's new. It was also nice that we already knew the building and some people in it, otherwise that first day might have been a bit unsettling, nosey neighbors aside.

As I waited for the elevator on that first day, there was a note taped between the two lifts. The note read in Croatian:

In the hallway on the 8th floor there is a large, green parrot if someone in the building has lost him come and get him.

Wait? What? The note was in Croatian and I wasn't sure I had translated it right. Maybe "parrot" had another meaning like… keys, or wallet. You know something that could be easily, and *reasonably* lost or misplaced. I waited for Vana to come in from the car.

"Nope, that means parrot." As she said these words we both kind of looked at each other, and then our eyes slowly gazed upward as if trying to peer through the layers of concrete, up to the 8th floor. Was their really a green parrot flying around up there?

The elevator arrived and we shoved our stuff inside.

"How do you 'lose' a large parrot?" I asked.

"And not realize it?" Vana added. Somewhere, someone in that building was siting in an apartment thinking, *You know, it's awfully quiet today.*

Where a lot of neighborhoods in Croatia feel like a village, I guess my childhood neighborhood felt more like a garage. If I think back I can remember knowing a few of our neighbor's faces, but mostly we knew their cars. We would only see them pull into the driveway, park, and walk to the house. So, out of ten families living on the block, I could recognize about 20 cars. Save for the neighbors across the street, whose daughter was one of my best friends, when I was outside, playing in the front lawn, I maybe got a wave from the car to their front door, but that was about it (and there was certainly no old lady bench).

Meanwhile, walking through our Zagreb neighborhood feels like I'm strolling through the *Beatles* song "Penny Lane." Only where he sings that there is a barber showing photographs of haircuts, I see my hairdresser having a cigarette, I see the store clerk receiving an order, the girl in the bakery waves as I pass by. In the two cafes where we often meet with our friends everyone knows us, and which kid we belong to.

And the kids treat the space around the cafes and the little park like it's theirs. If I contrast this to my childhood, I see all of us confined to our own backyards. And for a while I despaired that I wouldn't be giving my daughter the American dream: a house and a yard.

But I now I see that her whole time playing outside doesn't involve playing in a lonely fenced-in yard, but rampaging with her friends across half a neighborhood, running passed familiar places and faces without a second glance, and like a bunch of kid-powered electrons racing around a single atom, but still a part of that atom, they are a part of that community.

In the vast expanse of the American midwest, we move through so many houses and neighborhoods that we remain anonymous. And like an antidote to familiarity, anonymity breeds indifference and indifference is the antithesis to community. And what I've learned through our epic apartment hunt, through the searching, the buying, the worrying, the hoping that the deal would go through, is that this is the biggest difference between here and there, between my Croatia and my America.

And so, after the end of the arduous process of home buying, the bureaucracy, the reluctance of people to close a deal, I was relieved that we'd moved within our neighborhood, to a building where we already had friends, and where we were already familiar with the faces of the people we didn't know. It felt like home the first night, which we all spent sleeping in the same room... in the same bed (*sigh*). Who could ask for anything more than that? And there's even a strong chance that we could become acquainted with a large, green parrot.

CHAPTER 16

Questions about America

One evening, while on vacation (if you call staying with your mother-in-law "vacation") we were walking past a bank in Split with it's alarm going off. We didn't see any hooded men with bags of money running out, or any obvious get-away car idling by the curb, so it looked like it was just a malfunction of the alarm. Any minute we expected to see the police pull up, but by the time we made it to the intersection down the street the alarm seemed to be blaring and the lights flashing in vain because no police showed up.

Somehow all of this brought up the conversation of alarms because Sara asked,

"What's an alarm?"

"It's a thing that makes a loud noise when someone breaks into your house or a bank or store or something," I replied. Sara grew a bit serious, then a bit inquisitive.

"Why would someone break into your house?" I realized this thought had never even crossed her mind. I didn't know what to say. I decided to be honest.

"Sometimes, thieves, bad people, break into people's houses to steal things."

"Like my toys?"

"Well, more like money or jewelry or something."

"Do we have an alarm?"

"No."

"Then someone could break into our apartment." Now I'd done it and I had to fix it.

"Listen, no one is going to break into our apartment. First, you know that big, heavy door we have? That's a security door and it deters people from breaking in because it's hard to break into. Second, even if someone did break into our house, they would be very disappointed about what they found inside: a bunch of books, a not very expensive TV, an old PS3, and what else…

"Legos."

"Yes, Legos" (although if you know anything about Legos, those things are damn expensive).

"But you said you had an alarm on your house in America." *Did I? Damn it!*

"Um… yeah… we did, but that's different because it's a lot easier to break into houses in America. Do you know how many doors my house had? Five. Five doors that someone could break into. Most houses have a least two. And how many doors does our apartment have?

"One."

"Yes, one really big, really strong door. Also in the US houses have lots of windows that someone could break into, and so it's real easy to break into a house in America, so we have alarms."

"We have windows," Sara replied. Arrrgh!

"Yes, we too have windows, but you'd have to climb out on the side of a high building to get through our windows, which no one is going to do because they know that there is nothing that valuable in our apartment." I braced myself, recalling how the logic of the ladder scaling crocodile did little to assuage Sara's fear of the dark and any lurking crocodiles a dim room might contain. Would she challenge my hypothesis on thieves, windows, and the height of our apartment with her own theory?

"Oh. Good." Apparently not, *whew*.

"Right. Plus the neighbors would see them, or hear them. And if they can't get the front door open because it's locked, are they going to try to steal our TV out of the window?"

"No, I guess not. That would be silly."

Yes! Yes that would be silly! Situation calmed.

"Daddy, did anyone ever break into your house in America?"

"No... Well... wait. Yeah. One time a guy was trying to break into our house and my dad caught him, but while he waited for the police he got away."

"How did he get away?"

"He asked my dad for a glass of water, my dad gave it to him and then he threw it at him and ran away."

"Oh. That's not good."

"No, but he never came back."

And then we begin one of Sara's new favorite things: Questions about violence in America. When she was younger and I would put her to bed, she always wanted me to tell her about wild animals that I'd seen. And since I was from Oklahoma, I'd seen quite a few. Deer, foxes, a skunk, several snakes, two tarantulas, raccoons, possums, an alligator (in Louisiana). And... (sigh) just now am I beginning to understand where her fear of crocodiles might've come from. So, after this conversation in Split, she wanted me to tell her about crime and criminals in America.

Let me just say that one of biggest fears in my life is that, like many Croatians, my daughter will move to a different country. I can accept it if she moves to somewhere in Europe. As long as it's a short plane ride or a fascinating car ride away (castles people, never under estimate the allure of seeing castles by the side of the road, and in Europe they are everywhere), I'm fine with it. But, I do not want her to live in the US. Not because of the crime, but just because of the distance. Ironic, right? I live faraway from my parents and family, and yet I'm worried that my daughter will do the same thing. So, maybe it's not such a bad idea to tell her about crime in the US at such a young age...

As I'm trying to get her to fall asleep and she's asking me questions, I'm simultaneously balancing what to censor and sanitize, while trying to think of enough things to keep me talking, while (yawn) trying not to fall asleep myself. It's at those times, in those in between instances that you can unlock and remember all kinds of things you forgot.

Somehow we get on the topic of motion activated lights. Our old, rented apartment had had one above the front door, and while growing up in Tulsa, our neighbor installed one above his driveway. I had always remembered the light because it shinned directly into my bedroom, but I'd forgotten the story behind the light until Sara asks me about it.

When I was five years old the neighbor, who was a judge, came over and told my parents about the light and why he was installing it. A few nights before the house behind his had been burglarized by armed men. After committing the crime, they jumped the fence into our neighbor's backyard and then ran down the driveway to the street, where presumably they had parked their car or a car was waiting for them. Now, I don't know if anyone was hurt in this event or if anyone was in the burgled house. But, I know and I remember hearing that one of the bits of evidence that all this transpired were the bullets that had fallen out of the thieves pockets and our neighbor, the judge, found the next morning in his driveway.

Laying there next to Sara, this memory blows my mind. Armed men ran past our house in the dead of night and it seemed just normal? And we lived in one of the city's nicest neighborhoods. I mean we LIVED NEXT TO A JUDGE! I don't remember my parents being overly concerned, I just remember the judge installing the motion light on the side of his house. Although I'm not sure what good it would have done anyone, other than I guess deter them from using his driveway as an escape route again.

I tell Sara about the police helicopter that flies around the city, shining a spotlight everywhere when it's looking for a suspect. I go on to tell her about the time it was above our neighborhood, flying around, highlighting the neighbors' back yards and front yards before pouring its bleaching rays through my own bedroom window (which was super exciting!)

She keeps asking me, "What else?"

I tell her how sometimes at my friend's house we would forget the alarm was on and open a door to let the dog out, or the cat in. Then the alarm would go off and my friend would have to run to the keypad and type in the code and then wait for the call from the security company and give a secret password.

I don't tell her about living at my dad's house and watching what was a nice neighborhood near the historic Route 66 descend into a mess of drunks, drugs, and prostitution. And since I'd grown up on Route 66, my friend who worked for the US Embassy and was organizing a Route 66 festival in Zagreb asked if I would write about it for my blog.

"Are you sure you? Because Route 66 in Tulsa is where most of the prostitutes are, it's also where you can probably score some meth or heroine?"

"Um... could you refrain from those details and capture more *the spirit* of Route 66."

I knew what she was saying, so I didn't write or tell Sara about the time my parents watched a drunk biker try and break into a house across the driveway from our duplex. The man was trying to kick the door in, and was nearly through when the police arrived. The resident told the guy that he was one second from getting his head blown off. While the biker was trying to break in, the occupant had a 12 gauge shotgun pointed at the door, and was on the phone with the police. Had the man succeeded in busting through the door, the owner, and according to my father there wasn't an ounce of uncertainty in this man's statement, would have "blown the biker away."

Finally, Sara falls asleep and I lay beside her thinking how strange all of this sounds to her. Alarms, spotlights, armed break-ins, police, the trappings of my childhood are strange artifacts for hers. In the last book I wrote about how

I imagined Croatia to be unsafe before I moved here ("Balkans," "War," etc...), but how it is incredibly safe. Three years later and I still can't get over this fact.

To me one of the main reasons for this difference is the amount of social trust in Croatia and America. Here, kids walk home, or ride public transit from school, alone, at age 10. Why? Because school gets out at 13:30. And I know that in no time, I'll have to let Sara walk home from school. Last year I saw a Mirko's oldest daughter and her two friends walking down the street at 13:45. I did a double-take and asked, "What are you doing?" I thought maybe I'd caught them skipping class. Aha!

"Schools out," they replied. "We're going home." I'd forgotten this could happen. Now I know that it will take a lot of trust and faith to let my daughter spend unsupervised time with her friends, but she will... and that trust won't just exist between my daughter and myself. To let your 10-year-old kid walk around unsupervised requires that you trust all the people that you don't know. It requires that you trust society.

I feel that in the US we've lost that social trust. Maybe it's because people like me remember all these things from their childhood. Or all the stories of child abductions that plagued the 1980s and 1990s. Or maybe it's from shows like *Unsolved Mysteries,* which was the scariest show to ever air on TV. Statistically, crime in America is at an all time low. For example, in 2014 New York saw 216 less murders than it did in 1965, but to many Americans, 1965 marks the "good-ole days." I would never have thought that 2014 was safer than 1965. I think this is largely due to the country's diminished faith in its society.

In Croatia the odd thing is that amid all the corruption, the public's skepticism towards the country's leaders and politicians, the general pessimism that comes with doing... well, anything, I feel like there is quite a bit of trust in the society. It might come from the nosy old ladies, the neighbors, or the regularity with which we meet and greet the same faces.

The normalcy of this way of life in Croatia, one that makes alarms, guns, and police helicopters seem abnormal, is one of the stranger and more beautiful things about living here. And if all those elements of crime and violence are mere accouterments used for, albeit, odd bedtime stories for my daughter, then that's fine with me.

CHAPTER 17

How to play "Croatia the Board Game"

In 2015 my sister and her husband came to visit us. One of the things I love about having different family members visit Croatia is that they immediately understand why we've chosen to live here. Of course they have their lives and careers back home, so it's not like they are dying to move here too, but they "get it." And they say,

"Cody, I get it. I get why you like living here."

They probably "get it" because their visit consists of having coffee in the square, walking through the safe and historic streets of Zagreb, having me drive them to the beautiful coast, and eating soup at punica's. All the bureaucratic and pessimistic frustrations aside, these are the essential rudiments of our daily life (save for the frequent visits to the coast, for those of us who don't live on the sea). And when you look at it like that... really, what's not to "get?"

Anyway, during their stay they introduced us to playing boardgames. Yes, boardgames. And just a real quick note: when I say boardgames in Croatia, most people say, "You mean like *Čovječe ne ljuti se*?" This game in question, translated as "*Man, Don't Be Angry*," is the equivalent to the game in the US called *Sorry*. And this is hilarious because Croatians don't really ever say sorry. Well, actually they do say *"sori,"* but that doesn't mean what you might think it means. If a Croatian says *"sori,"* what she really means is "whatever, get over it." *Oprostite* is the Croatian word for apologizing. But this can be used as like *"excuse me, I'm trying to wedge myself passed you on a crowded tram,"* or it can be used like *"Oh, sorry I said something rude to you about your soup, again."* The ubiquitous use of *oprostite* and the lack of a genuine apology with *sori* makes most apologies feel like they fall a bit short. The fact that a game called *Sorry* is called *Man, Don't Be Angry* in Croatia is illustrative of the differences between the American and Croatian perspectives in many ways. In the US we apologize for things we aren't really sorry for, or we try to be sorry for things we shouldn't be, like playing a game. While Croatians, just sort of call it like it is. It's a game. Don't be angry, man!

OK, back to boardgames. The games we play are a bit more complicated than *Sorry* (or call it *Čovječe ne ljuti se*, whatever). One game is about building roads and castles in medieval France, another one is about having to cooperate in order to escape a cursed, sinking island, and still some others are about making sandwiches, preventing the coming of Cthulhu, launching a coup against the government, and fighting zombies. You know, good, family fun.

But all this got me thinking, what would *Croatia the Board Game* be like? We already have games that are essential *America the Board Game*, like *Monopoly* and *The Game of Life*. The goal and the key to winning each game is to make the most money… and that pretty much sums up American life and society. If you look at how the American system is geared, how the machinery runs and hums, what it shapes and molds most of our goals into, then we see that the goals of these games are not really that far removed from the US's reality.

Really? Think about it. *Really?* Yes, Really. *Really.*

So what then would be the goal of *Croatia the Board Game*? And how would you win? Perhaps more importantly, what kind of game would it be? There are competitive games where you play against the other players, like *Monopoly*. There are cooperative games where you and the other players work to defeat the game, like the one we have about a cursed, sinking island. Everyone has to work together or they all die a horrible death at the bottom of the sea. And there are press-your-luck games where to win big you have to risk big. And there are bluffing games where you must pretend to be something you aren't or to have something you don't. So, which style of game fits Croatia?

Clearly, with our emphasis on individual initiative, success and wealth *America the Board Game* would be a competitive game. Given the importance of relationships, the social trust, the neighborly neighbors, the way friends and family look out for each other (even if that means being completely pessimistic and skeptical about some foreigner's wonderful ideas), and the overall sense of obligation to the ones you call friends, *Croatia the Board Game* would certainly be a cooperative game.

I can see it now: it's you and your *kum* (godparent and, or the best man, and or maid of honor), your friends, close neighbors and punica against the game itself, a world of well connected others, an impenetrable bureaucracy, and an unresponsive political system. But, and here's the catch, the rules of the "game" can both hinder and help you. You have to use the very things that adversely affect you to win.

For all the times we complain about how a relationship can go before a rule, we've all been on both sides of that equation. Sometimes we are the ones standing in line, locked in the morass of officialdom, sometimes we are the ones bypassing that line, speeding like we're in the carpool lane, through the graces of a connection. It sucks, and it doesn't. And this is the Croatian paradox. What is the problem, is at other times the solution.

I don't mean just the use of "connections," but rather the positive and negative aspects about a society where the personal is given more weight than the official process. The thing that makes Croatia so different from the US (and elsewhere?), is the rigidness in which we, Americans, believe in the individual and her power to overcome all obstacles, alone. The more time I live in Croatia the more I realize how lonely and alienating the US can be. In 2004, 25 percent of Americans reported that they have no "social confidant" in whom they can confide and talk to. In 1985 that number was 10 percent. Americans are becoming more isolated. Whereas everything I've written about so far, the community built around my blog, the sage (though skeptical) advice of friends, the solidarity among my Croatian friends and family that comes with being beset with adverse circumstances, like when you can't find a job, when your publisher declares bankruptcy or when you're trying to buy a spatially undefined apartment, and the familiarity of neighbors, all paints a picture of a place in which we are always, ever aware of being socially interconnected. In a way Croatia works like social media before there was any social media. I mean before *Instagram* was a thing and people began taking pictures of their food, your Croatian neighbors likely knew what you ate for lunch anyway. It was either a topic of conversation among the wise old ladies on the bench, they saw you lugging the groceries home, or they just smelled it cooking across the hallway. And I believe that all of this connectedness prevents Croatia's problems from becoming bigger problems, while also being the source of our problems to begin with.

So, I imagine a board game where you build social capital and better connections by having coffee with each other, where you engage in acts of reciprocity between friends, and little by little use the connections you've made through such behavior to navigate the world of Croatia. How this game would be played, with dice, cards or something else, I don't know. At times the connections you make enable you to do simple things, like get a doctor's appointment, but where you still have to wait in line at the doctor's office (consider this like a minor use of a connection). At other times in the game, if you've played your connections right, you can open doors previously closed to you. And finally, the big question, as you become more and more connected, how will you use your power? Will you use it for good or for ill? As you become more and more integrated and connected within the society, will you use your influence to help qualified, hard-working people left out of the loop find work? Or will you use your power to employ your idiot cousins in jobs where they don't have to do anything, but get paid three times more than the average Croatian's wage? Will you wield the power of connections for your own corrupt, self-interests, benefiting your cronies? Or will you use the importance of social ties to try and better Croatian society as a whole?

As I'm ever the optimist, I feel like this board game is being played for real and there are two ways to play it: one positive, and one negative. A lot of people in this country use the ties of family and friendship in ways that serve to correct the deficiencies of the social, political, and economic system. For whatever reason, in order to be taken seriously as a candidate for a job, you often need a connection. This means you can't just apply for a job or walk in and say, "hire me" based solely on your qualifications (or maybe you can, it's just rarely tried. In fact I know someone who just got a job and purposely didn't use any connections). But, I think of this type of "connection" as a reference or a first phase recommendation. I know people who have gotten jobs through friends. I have friends who have gotten jobs for people via this first type of connection. So-and-so is looking for work, and some work is looking for someone. I also know that the people in our circle of connections are capable and competent. Rather than see this as a problem, I see it as a way in which Croatia avoids the atomized loneliness of America. These types of connections put good people in good places and increase the social bonds that make Croatia so different than the US. These types of actions are the duty of friends, and the ties among neighbors. They make Croatia a stronger society than other ones that are out there in the world.

Of course, the downside are the types of connections that everyone speaks about with disdain. These are the "favors" used more for political rather than personal points. These are the dead end, do nothing, redundant jobs, filled by the friends and family of the local elites. The jobs in the state sectors or the jobs where someone important offers some business to a firm, on the condition that they employ their third cousin, friend of a friend, or whomever. These people are the so-called *uhljebi* (a word I don't really know how to translate). And their actions are the very actions and behaviors that constrain Croatia's growth and progress, that weaken our laws, and compromise our future. They are the reason so many people are leaving Croatia.

So, in *Croatia the Board Game* you'd have a choice. Will you use the connections and thick society that exists in Croatia to better the society as a whole (and this includes to keep it from getting worse)? Or will you use them to better yourself and your select tribe? And at the end of the game there is no single winner. Rather, the players' actions and how they cooperate determine how many losers there will be. It's up to us and how we play. While in *America The Board Game* you have to have a clear winner (someone with the most money) and a bunch of losers (others with a little money), in *Croatia the Board Game* our actions in the game, who we help and how, will determine whether we have a lot, some, or a just a few losers.

I hope and believe that in the real life version of this game (and yes, it's a bit simplified) most of us want to have as few losers as possible. And for me, the Croatian paradox gives us the opportunity to play this game in such a way that together, most of us can win.

(And we *better* play it this way because I don't want my daughter to have to move to another country!)

CHAPTER 18

Boba Fetch and Tomorrow

During our whole apartment hunting um... adventure? Saga? Quest?, I kept promising Sara that as soon as we moved we would get a pet. She wanted either a guinea pig or a dog. And I wanted a dog because you know, man's best friend vs annoying, squeaky, pooping thing in a cage. And did you know that when a dog looks at you, he's actually hugging you with his eyes? Hugs. With. His. Eyes! It's true! Scientists did studies and the same part of a dog's brain lights up when he looks at you as does a human's brain when you get a hug. Now, when a cat looks at you, well, he's actually just trying to murder you... with his eyes![9]

Not soon after we moved, like even on the day of, Sara was asking

"Can we get a pet now?"

"Not yet, but soon."

"Can we get a pet now?"

"Can we get a pet now?"

---

[9] Sorry to offend any cat people out there. I love cats too.

"Can we get a pet now?"

"Can we get a pet now?"

By the time the autumn arrived there was nothing preventing us from getting a pet, other than you know, worrying about getting a pet. At the cafe near the little park where the kids played, I discussed getting a pet with the neighbors. Mirko and Vesna, Adrian and Marta, me and Vana, plus a few other parents all sat around like usual. Indeed, the regularity with which we came and sat at the cafe day in and day out made it seem like it was the bar from *Cheers*, a place where everybody knew my name. In a way my life was seemingly like a sitcom, awkward, funny, peppered with bouts of frustration. Tonight's episode: The Dog.

"I guess we're going to get a dog." I said. Vesna looked at me like, *come on, really? (Ma daj)*.

"It's not like in America, you live in an apartment now. You'll have to walk him in the morning," Adrian commented.

"That's all right…"

"Oh right, you like getting up early in the morning."

It's true, I do, and this makes everyone, save for punica, think I'm strange.

"But you know, when you're out in the rain and in the snow, walking the dog, we'll be pointing and saying, ah look…"

Clearly, Adrian and Marta have a cat.

Even punica adds her wisdom telling me that a dog is a big responsibility, that we'll have to take him with us everywhere, feed him, take him to the vet, and that if we get one from the shelter you never know *what kind* of dog it might be. And I listen, thinking, she knows I'm a parent, right? I mean a pet is like a kid you care about a little less.

But since we are near the end of this book, you and I now know that this skepticism is normal. Our friends and family were skeptical of getting a dog because they wanted to make sure we knew what we were getting into. Even Vana was a bit cautious. She seemed like someone standing on the edge of a pool, hesitant to jump in, but willing to do so eventually.

One Friday, she and I finally went to the animal shelter in Dumovec, a small (town?) just outside of Zagreb. There we saw hundreds of barking dogs of all shapes and sizes. Our intention was just to scope the scene and determine whether it would be too traumatic to bring Sara. Maybe she'd want to take ALL the dogs home. While we were looking at the small to medium size dogs, I noticed one calm dachshund being razzed and abused by the other dogs in his kennel. Having grown up as a shorter than average, left handed, dyslexic, un-athletic kid, who often found himself stuck in lockers and trashcans, I was sympathetic to this little guy's plight. Plus he seemed calm, which was the kind of dog I wanted. We just asked to see him, but when the worker put him in Vana's arms, that was it. Her skepticism evaporated, she'd jumped in that metaphorical pool, and the dog seemed to just melt into her arms, congealing into a puddle of wide human hugging-canine, shimmering eyes of gratitude. That afternoon, Sara finally got a pet. His name, Boba Fetch.[10]

In the US, at least in Oklahoma, when I was a kid, having a dog was not a social experience. We rarely walked our dog because he could just do his "business" in the backyard, and he didn't need the exercise because he just chased squirrels and us in the backyard. And that's how it seemed with all of my friends who also had dogs.

In Vrbik, however, it was a different story. If you want to talk to people, get a dog. If I had had a dog at the beginning of my Croatian adventure, then I would never have needed a blog. A friendly dog in Croatia is like your social ambassador. Everyone who sees him wants to pet him and he seems to want to be petted by everyone he sees. This leads to greetings, questions about the dog, then questions about me and before you know it I'm talking to people I wouldn't normally have talked to.

Boba Fetch also showed me how much the neighborhood knew about me beforehand. Whereas you (or I) might've thought that the them of Chapter Fourteen: "we are all familiar with each other in a community, and ain't it swell" was little too idealistic or imagined. Turns out, nope. At the store while buying dog food, the saleswoman says,

"Since when did you get a dog?"

At the park a kid I don't know says,

"I didn't know you all had a dog."

---

[10] Now, can there be a more fitting name for a dog at the end of a book called *Croatia Strikes Back?* For the three of you who haven't seen the Star Wars movie *The Empire Strikes Back*, Bobba Fett is the name of the awesome bounty hunter, who has a jetpack by the way, that tracks down Han Solo to the Cloud City of Bespin, where... oh never mind. Just see the film! For those of you who know what I'm talking about I have to give credit to Ana Jembrek who suggested this Star Wars themed name. She also suggest other options, like Chew Barka and Luke Skybarker. Genius!

In the elevator, a young woman, whom I've never spoken to, says to me, in English,

"Hey, you got a dog."

Yep, nothing like getting a pet to realize that the most of the neighborhood knew I was a dog-less foreigner (*What? You mean my Croatian disguise hasn't been fooling anyone?*). Just as we began treating Boba Fetch like a member of the family so did our friends. Gone was the skepticism of our pre-dog world. When Boba Fetch was sick one day, Vesna called and asked if he was OK. In the same way she would have called and ask about Sara. Over a beer Adrian petted him the whole time, holding his leash, praising how calm he was. The kids competed with who could walk him, especially Nora's older sister Violeta, who would help walk him with Vana. Mirko was talking about him to Vesna, all the way from Frankfurt where he was flying airplanes. Even when punica called each day, she asked about the dog and *then* she would asked about Sara. She seemed equally interested in what they had both eaten for lunch each day.

This. This is what I love about Croatia. Despite, or because of, the inept institutions, the labyrinthian bureaucracy, the corrupt politicians we have a tight society. At times it is in such stark contrast to America's worship of the individual, that the two almost eclipse each other. I often find myself oscillating between my native and adopted cultures, longing for one while also valuing the other. Here, your friends and family may preach a skeptical sermon and seem endlessly pessimistic, but once you decide on something, they support you in your decision. Whether it's buying an apartment, writing a book, applying for a job, marrying an American, or getting a dog. Where I might feel like saying "told you so" when a forewarned disaster befalls a friend, I believe our Croatian friends will just say, "I'm here, what do you need?"

It's around 6:15 on a grey morning. Autumn looms in the air. Wet drizzle spits from the sky, puddles have gathered overnight in the cracked and buckled concrete of our housing block. The sound of runoff plays through the rusted drains and gutters.

Boba Fetch and I walked around the back of the building where there is a large grassy area, unkept and overgrown. With my hood pulled up against the damp and a taste of the morning's instant coffee in my mouth, I reminisce about Adrian's warning that I'd being doing this every morning, because, well, I've been doing this every morning. And Boba Fetch is probably going to live for another 12 to 15 years.

As we walk on, the rain lets up. A few minutes later and the morning sun breaks through the clouds. The dawn-light reflects off the usually dull windows of the apartment building. The drooping weeds, glisten in the early morning light. *Actually,* I think, *I hope I'll be doing this for the next 12-15 years.* By that time so many unknowns will be known. Sara will be into early adulthood, we'll know if she's staying or leaving, we'll know about our jobs, we'll know what the then future holds, and we'll know how we, our friends and the country have faired. We'll know how we decided to play the Croatian game. And we'll know, finally, for certain how long we can survive in Croatia.

I look at the dawn through the thinning curtains of mist, and dare to hope that in 15 years I'll be walking our dog in the early chill of an autumn morning, just like this.

In some ways the dog and I are alike. At one point we were both strays, adrift, lost and lonely, and now we are both a part of the community.

Boba Fetch shakes off water from his fur. He sniffs and looks at me expectantly. I look up at the grey, brutalist monument, towering beside us, and imagine Sara and Vana still asleep in the dim light. They'll need to get up. I put aside my thoughts about tomorrow and decide to focus on the day ahead. Boba Fetch sniffs again.

"All right," I say. "Let's go home."

Author's note

This book is based on my experiences in Croatia. In order to protect the innocent, I've once again changed everyone's name, even the dog's! I've combined multiple people into a single composite, while completely making up other people. So, I guess it's best to say that this story "approximates" the truth. I know this tale barters in generalizations, and there are exceptions to every rule, but I believe that the spirit of the book is true, even if all the facts and everything else are less so.

Acknowledgements

There are a lot of people who have helped me survive in Croatia, more than they helped write this book, but you know the two go together. I'm eternally grateful to all of them. So, in no order of importance they are: My four parents, my three siblings, and all the other family members that send Sara things in the mail, the after school-playground-neighborhood-cafe club of parents and neighbors (you know who you are in this book), the neighbors in Split, and Alex Simmons, the dearly departed William Worrell, Zach Taylor, Philip the Bruce, Jake Tomsky, Vjeran Pavlaković, Dejan Jović, Zlatan Krajina, Viktorija Car, Saša Bijelobaba, Mirela Landsman Vinković, Daria Marjanović, Chris Bushill, Katya Miličić, Kristijan Nikolić, Ivana Bašić, Boris Jukić, Elizabeth Blumenthal, Johnathan Roberts and Tamara Tomić, The Boat of Culture, all of my colleagues at the Faculty of Political Science, and at the Voice of Croatia, the people at the US Embassy in Zagreb, past and present, my publisher Neven Antičević and Ana Silić, and of course everyone who bought, reviewed, and recommended the first book, read, liked, shared or commented on my blog, especially Nermina, and of course my Croatian family, the ever vigilant punica, my amazing, creative daughter, who hopefully won't resent what I wrote about her here when she's 13, and my wife, who remains my biggest fan, harshest critic, and best friend.

Printed in Great Britain
by Amazon